D1611118

Just The

facts101
Textbook Key Facts

Textbook Outlines, Highlights, and Practice Quizzes

Discovering Statistics Using IBM SPSS Statistics: And Sex and Drugs and Rock 'n' Roll

by Andy P. Field, 4th Edition

All "Just the Facts101" Material Written or Prepared by Cram101 Publishing

Title Page

Visit Cram101.com for full Practice Exams

"Just the Facts101" is a Cram101 publication and tool designed to give you all the facts from your textbooks. Visit Cram101.com for the full practice test for each of your chapters for virtually any of your textbooks.

Cram101 has built custom study tools specific to your textbook. We provide all of the factual testable information and unlike traditional study guides, we will never send you back to your textbook for more information.

YOU WILL NEVER HAVE TO HIGHLIGHT A BOOK AGAIN!

Cram101 StudyGuides

All of the information in this StudyGuide is written specifically for your textbook. We include the key terms, places, people, and concepts... the information you can expect on your next exam!

Want to take a practice test?

Throughout each chapter of this StudyGuide you will find links to cram101.com where you can select specific chapters to take a complete test on, or you can subscribe and get practice tests for up to 12 of your textbooks, along with other exclusive cram101.com tools like problem solving labs and reference libraries.

Cram101.com

Only cram101.com gives you the outlines, highlights, and PRACTICE TESTS specific to your textbook. Cram101.com is an online application where you'll discover study tools designed to make the most of your limited study time.

By purchasing this book, you get 50% off the normal monthly subscription fee!. Just enter the promotional code **'DK73DW21776'** on the Cram101.com registration screen.

www.Cram101.com

Learning System

facts101

Discovering Statistics Using IBM SPSS Statistics: And Sex and Drugs and Rock 'n' Roll
Andy P. Field, 4th

CONTENTS

Chapter 1. Why is my evil lecturer forcing me to learn statistics?

5

Coefficient

ANOVA

Categorical data

Continuity correction

Q-Q plot

Data analysis

Data collection

Test statistic

Big Brother

Variable

Levene's test

Bar chart

SPSS

Chi-square test

Dependent variable

Independent variable

Odds ratio

Raw score

Binary variable

Chapter 1. Why is my evil lecturer forcing me to learn statistics?

CHAPTER OUTLINE: KEY TERMS, PEOPLE, PLACES, CONCEPTS

_____ | Factorial ANOVA

_____ | Levels of measurement

_____ | Outcome

_____ | Discrete probability distributions

_____ | Factor analysis

_____ | Concurrent validity

_____ | Criterion validity

_____ | Predictive validity

_____ | Reliability

_____ | Validity

_____ | Cronbach's alpha

_____ | English

_____ | Content validity

_____ | Ecological validity

_____ | Repeatability

_____ | David Hume

_____ | Causality

_____ | Confounding

_____ | Hypothetico-deductive model

Chapter 1. Why is my evil lecturer forcing me to learn statistics?

7

CHAPTER OUTLINE: KEY TERMS, PEOPLE, PLACES, CONCEPTS

Variation

Bonferroni correction

Precision

Practice effect

Randomization

Frequency distribution

Histogram

Logistic regression

Normal distribution

Kurtosis

Negative skew

Platykurtic distribution

Positive skew

Sphericity

Bimodal distribution

Central tendency

Centre

Mode

Median

Chapter 1. Why is my evil lecturer forcing me to learn statistics?
CHAPTER OUTLINE: KEY TERMS, PEOPLE, PLACES, CONCEPTS

Multimodal distribution

Distribution

Interquartile range

Lower quartile

Quartile

Second quartile

Third quartile

Deviance

Percentile

Quantile

Deviation

Variance

Standard deviation

Probability distribution

Density function

Probability density function

Statistical model

Standard error

Presentation Layer

Chapter 1. Why is my evil lecturer forcing me to learn statistics?

9

CHAPTER OUTLINE: KEY TERMS, PEOPLE, PLACES, CONCEPTS

| | Wright |

CHAPTER HIGHLIGHTS & NOTES: KEY TERMS, PEOPLE, PLACES, CONCEPTS

Coefficient	In mathematics, a Coefficient is a multiplicative factor in some term of an expression (or of a series); it is usually a number, but in any case does not involve any variables of the expression. For instance in

$$7x^2 - 3xy + 1.5 + y$$

the first three terms respectively have Coefficients 7, −3, and 1.5 (in the third term there are no variables, so the Coefficient is the term itself; it is called the constant term or constant Coefficient of this expression). The final term does not have any explicitly written Coefficient, but is usually considered to have Coefficient 1, since multiplying by that factor would not change the term.

ANOVA	In statistics, ANOVA is a collection of statistical models, and their associated procedures, in which the observed variance is partitioned into components due to different sources of variation. In its simplest form ANOVA provides a statistical test of whether or not the means of several groups are all equal, and therefore generalizes Student's two-sample t-test to more than two groups. ANOVAs are helpful because they possess a certain advantage over a two-sample t-test. Doing multiple two-sample t-tests would result in a largely increased chance of committing a type I error. For this reason, ANOVAs are useful in comparing three or more means.

There are three conceptual classes of such models:

· Fixed-effects models assume that the data came from normal populations which may differ only in their means. (Model 1) · Random effects models assume that the data describe a hierarchy of different populations whose differences are constrained by the hierarchy. (Model 2) · Mixed-effect models describe the situations where both fixed and random effects are present. (Model 3)

Categorical data	In statistics, categorical data is that part of an observed dataset that consists of categorical variables, or for data that has been converted into that form, for example as grouped data.

Chapter 1. Why is my evil lecturer forcing me to learn statistics?

CHAPTER HIGHLIGHTS & NOTES: KEY TERMS, PEOPLE, PLACES, CONCEPTS

	More specifically, categorical data may derive from either or both of observations made of qualitative data, where the observations are summarised as counts or cross tabulations, or of quantitative data, where observations might be directly observed counts of events happening or they might counts of values that occur within given intervals. Often, purely categorical data are summarised in the form of a contingency table.
Continuity correction	In probability theory, if a random variable X has a binomial distribution with parameters n and p, i.e., X is distributed as the number of 'successes' in n independent Bernoulli trials with probability p of success on each trial, then $P(X \leq x) = P(X < x + 1)$ for any x ∈ {0, 1, 2, ... n}. If np and n(1 − p) are large (sometimes taken to mean ≥ 5), then the probability above is fairly well approximated by $P(Y \leq x + 1/2)$ where Y is a normally distributed random variable with the same expected value and the same variance as X, i.e., E(Y) = np and var(Y) = np(1 − p). This addition of 1/2 to x is a continuity correction.
Q-Q plot	In statistics, a Q-Q plot is a probability plot, which is a graphical method for comparing two probability distributions by plotting their quantiles against each other. First, the set of intervals for the quantiles are chosen. A point (x,y) on the plot corresponds to one of the quantiles of the second distribution (y-coordinate) plotted against the same quantile of the first distribution (x-coordinate).
Data analysis	Analysis of data is a process of inspecting, cleaning, transforming, and modeling data with the goal of highlighting useful information, suggesting conclusions, and supporting decision making. Data analysis has multiple facets and approaches, encompassing diverse techniques under a variety of names, in different business, science, and social science domains. Data mining is a particular data analysis technique that focuses on modeling and knowledge discovery for predictive rather than purely descriptive purposes.
Data collection	Data collection is a term used to describe a process of preparing and collecting data - for example as part of a process improvement or similar project. The purpose of data collection is to obtain information to keep on record, to make decisions about important issues, to pass information on to others. Primarily, data is collected to provide information regarding a specific topic.

Chapter 1. Why is my evil lecturer forcing me to learn statistics?

11

CHAPTER HIGHLIGHTS & NOTES: KEY TERMS, PEOPLE, PLACES, CONCEPTS

Test statistic	In statistical hypothesis testing, a hypothesis test is typically specified in terms of a test statistic, which is a function of the sample; it is considered as a numerical summary of a set of data that reduces the data to one or a small number of values that can be used to perform a hypothesis test. Given a null hypothesis and a test statistic T, we can specify a 'null value' T_0 such that values of T close to T_0 present the strongest evidence in favor of the null hypothesis, whereas values of T far from T_0 present the strongest evidence against the null hypothesis. An important property of a test statistic is that we must be able to determine its sampling distribution under the null hypothesis, which allows us to calculate p-values.
Big Brother	Big Brother (alias BB) is a tool for systems and network monitoring, generally used by system administrators. The advent of the dynamic web page allowed Big Brother to be one of the first monitoring systems to use the web as its user interface. Prior to this, monitoring tools were generally console based, or required graphic terminals such as X Window to operate.
Variable	In mathematics, a variable is a value that may change within the scope of a given problem or set of operations. In contrast, a constant is a value that remains unchanged, though often unknown or undetermined. The concepts of constants and variables are fundamental to many areas of mathematics and its applications.
Levene's test	In statistics, Levene's test is an inferential statistic used to assess the equality of variances in different samples. Some common statistical procedures assume that variances of the populations from which different samples are drawn are equal. Levene's test assesses this assumption.
Bar chart	A bar chart is a chart with rectangular bars with lengths proportional to the values that they represent. The bars can be plotted vertically or horizontally. A vertical bar chart is sometimes called a column bar chart.
SPSS	SPSS Statistics is a software package used for statistical analysis. It is now officially named 'IBM SPSS Statistics'. Companion products in the same family are used for survey authoring and deployment (IBM SPSS Data Collection), data mining (IBM SPSS Modeler), text analytics, and collaboration and deployment (batch and automated scoring services).
Chi-square test	A chi-square test is any statistical hypothesis test in which the sampling distribution of the test statistic is a chi-square distribution when the null hypothesis is true, or any in which this is asymptotically true, meaning that the sampling distribution (if the null hypothesis is true) can be made to approximate a chi-square distribution as closely as desired by making the sample size large enough.

Chapter 1. Why is my evil lecturer forcing me to learn statistics?

CHAPTER HIGHLIGHTS & NOTES: KEY TERMS, PEOPLE, PLACES, CONCEPTS

Some examples of chi-squared tests where the chi-square distribution is only approximately valid:•Pearson's chi-square test, also known as the chi-square goodness-of-fit test or chi-square test for independence. When mentioned without any modifiers or without other precluding context, this test is usually understood .•Yates' chi-square test, also known as Yates' correction for continuity•Mantel-Haenszel chi-square test.•Linear-by-linear association chi-square test.•The portmanteau test in time-series analysis, testing for the presence of autocorrelation•Likelihood-ratio tests in general statistical modelling, for testing whether there is evidence of the need to move from a simple model to a more complicated one (where the simple model is nested within the complicated one).

One case where the distribution of the test statistic is an exact chi-square distribution is the test that the variance of a normally-distributed population has a given value based on a sample variance.

Dependent variable	The terms 'dependent variable' and 'independent variable' are used in similar but subtly different ways in mathematics and statistics as part of the standard terminology in those subjects. They are used to distinguish between two types of quantities being considered, separating them into those available at the start of a process and those being created by it, where the latter (dependent variables) are dependent on the former (independent variables).
	The independent variable is typically the variable being manipulated or changed and the dependent variable is the observed result of the independent variable being manipulated.
Independent variable	The terms 'dependent variable' and 'Independent variable' are used in similar but subtly different ways in mathematics and statistics as part of the standard terminology in those subjects. They are used to distinguish between two types of quantities being considered, separating them into those available at the start of a process and those being created by it, where the latter (dependent variables) are dependent on the former (Independent variables).
	The Independent variable is typically the variable being manipulated or changed and the dependent variable is the observed result of the Independent variable being manipulated.
Odds ratio	The odds ratio is a measure of effect size, describing the strength of association or non-independence between two binary data values. It is used as a descriptive statistic, and plays an important role in logistic regression. Unlike other measures of association for paired binary data such as the relative risk, the odds ratio treats the two variables being compared symmetrically, and can be estimated using some types of non-random samples.
Raw score	In statistics and data analysis, a raw score is an original datum that has not been transformed.

Chapter 1. Why is my evil lecturer forcing me to learn statistics?

13

CHAPTER HIGHLIGHTS & NOTES: KEY TERMS, PEOPLE, PLACES, CONCEPTS

	This may include, for example, the original result obtained by a student on a test (i.e., the number of correctly answered items) as opposed to that score after transformation to a standard score or percentile rank or the like.
	Often the conversion must be made to a standard score before the data can be used.
Binary variable	The term binary data has various meanings in different technical fields. In general, it refers to a unit of data which can take on only two possible values, traditionally termed 0 and 1 in accordance with the binary numeral system. Related concepts in various fields are *logical value in logic, which represents the truth or falsehood of a logical proposition•Boolean value, a representation of the concepts 'true' or 'false' used to do Boolean arithmetic in logic and computer science•binary digit, a single 0 or 1 in a binary number, used to represent numbers in base 2 (the binary numeral system) In statistics
	In statistics, binary data is a statistical data type described by binary variables, which can take only two possible values.
Factorial ANOVA	Factorial ANOVA is used when the experimenter wants to study the effects of two or more treatment variables. The most commonly used type of Factorial ANOVA is the 2^2 (read 'two by two') design, where there are two independent variables and each variable has two levels or distinct values. However, such use of ANOVA for analysis of 2^k factorial designs and fractional factorial designs is 'confusing and makes little sense'; instead it is suggested to refer the value of the effect divided by its standard error to a t-table. Factorial ANOVA can also be multi-level such as 3^3, etc. or higher order such as 2×2×2, etc.. Since the introduction of data analytic software, the utilization of higher order designs and analyses has become quite common.
Levels of measurement	The 'levels of measurement', or scales of measure are expressions that typically refer to the theory of scale types developed by the psychologist Stanley Smith Stevens In that article, Stevens claimed that all measurement in science was conducted using four different types of scales that he called 'nominal', 'ordinal', 'interval' and 'ratio'.
Outcome	In game theory, an outcome is a set of moves or strategies taken by the players, or it is their payoffs resulting from the actions or strategies taken by all players. The two are complementary in that, given knowledge of the set of strategies of all players, the final state of the game is known, as are any relevant payoffs. In a game where chance or a random event is involved, the outcome is not known from only the set of strategies, but is only realized when the random event(s) are realized.
Discrete probability distributions	Discrete probability distributions arise in the mathematical description of probabilistic and statistical problems in which the values that might be observed are restricted to being within a pre-defined list of possible values.

	This list has either a finite number of members, or at most is countable.
	In probability theory, a probability distribution is called discrete if it is characterized by a probability mass function.
Factor analysis	Factor analysis is a statistical method used to describe variability among observed, correlated variables in terms of a potentially lower number of unobserved variables called factors. In other words, it is possible, for example, that variations in three or four observed variables mainly reflect the variations in fewer unobserved variables. Factor analysis searches for such joint variations in response to unobserved latent variables.
Concurrent validity	Concurrent validity is a parameter used in sociology, psychology, and other psychometric or behavioral sciences. Concurrent validity is demonstrated where a test correlates well with a measure that has previously been validated. The two measures may be for the same construct, or for different, but presumably related, constructs.
Criterion validity	In psychometrics, criterion validity is a measure of how well one variable or set of variables predicts an outcome based on information from other variables, and will be achieved if a set of measures from a personality test relate to a behavioral criterion on which psychologists agree. A typical way to achieve this is in relation to the extent to which a score on a personality test can predict future performance or behavior. Another way involves correlating test scores with another established test that also measures the same personality characteristic.
Predictive validity	In psychometrics, predictive validity is the extent to which a score on a scale or test predicts scores on some criterion measure.
	For example, the validity of a cognitive test for job performance is the correlation between test scores and, for example, supervisor performance ratings. Such a cognitive test would have predictive validity if the observed correlation were statistically significant.
Reliability	In statistics, reliability refers to the consistency of a measure. A measure is said to have a high reliability if it produces consistent results under consistent conditions. For example, measurements of people's height and weight are often extremely reliable.
Validity	In science and statistics, validity has no single agreed definition but generally refers to the extent to which a concept, conclusion or measurement is well-founded and corresponds accurately to the real world. The word 'valid' is derived from the Latin validus, meaning strong. The validity of a measurement tool (for example, a test in education) is considered to be the degree to which the tool measures what it claims to measure.
Cronbach's alpha	Cronbach's α (alpha) is a coefficient of reliability.

Chapter 1. Why is my evil lecturer forcing me to learn statistics?

15

CHAPTER HIGHLIGHTS & NOTES: KEY TERMS, PEOPLE, PLACES, CONCEPTS

It is commonly used as a measure of the internal consistency or reliability of a psychometric test score for a sample of examinees. It was first named alpha by Lee Cronbach in 1951, as he had intended to continue with further coefficients. The measure can be viewed as an extension of the Kuder-Richardson Formula 20 (KR-20), which is an equivalent measure for dichotomous items. Alpha is not robust against missing data. Several other Greek letters have been used by later researchers to designate other measures used in a similar context. Somewhat related is the average variance extracted (AVE).

Cronbach's α is defined as

$$\alpha = \frac{K}{K-1} \left(1 - \frac{\sum_{i=1}^{K} \sigma_{Y_i}^2}{\sigma_X^2} \right)$$

where K is the number of components (K-items or testlets), σ_X^2 the variance of the observed total test scores, and $\sigma_{Y_i}^2$ the variance of component i for the current sample of persons.

Alternatively, the Cronbach's α can also be defined as

$$\alpha = \frac{K\bar{c}}{(\bar{v} + (K-1)\bar{c})}$$

where K is as above, $\bar{v}$ the average variance, and $\bar{c}$ the average of all covariances between the components across the current sample of persons.

The standardized Cronbach's alpha can be defined as

$$\alpha_{\text{standardized}} = \frac{K\bar{r}}{(1 + (K-1)\bar{r})}$$

where K is as above and $\bar{r}$ the mean of the K(K − 1) / 2 non-redundant correlation coefficients (i.e., the mean of an upper triangular, or lower triangular, correlation matrix).

English

English is a database retrieval and reporting language somewhat like SQL, but with no programming or update abilities. It was originally released by Microdata in 1973 and named so that the company's brochures could claim that developers could generate reports on their implementation of the Pick operating system using English.

Content validity

In psychometrics, content validity refers to the extent to which a measure represents all facets of a given social construct. For example, a depression scale may lack content validity if it only assesses the affective dimension of depression but fails to take into account the behavioral dimension.

Chapter 1. Why is my evil lecturer forcing me to learn statistics?

Ecological validity	Ecological validity is a form of validity in a research study. For a research study to have ecological validity, the methods, materials and setting of the study must approximate the real-world that is being examined. Unlike internal and external validity, ecological validity is not necessary to the overall validity of a study.
Repeatability	Repeatability is the variation in measurements taken by a single person or instrument on the same item and under the same conditions. A less-than-perfect test-retest reliability causes test-retest variability. Such variability can be caused by, for example, intra-individual variability and intra-observer variability.
David Hume	David Hume was a Scottish philosopher, historian, economist, and essayist, known especially for his philosophical empiricism and skepticism. He is regarded as one of the most important figures in the history of Western philosophy and the Scottish Enlightenment. Hume is often grouped with John Locke, George Berkeley, and a handful of others as a British Empiricist.
Causality	Causality is the relationship between an event (the cause) and a second event (the effect), where the second event is understood as a consequence of the first.
	In common usage, causality is also the relationship between a set of factors (causes) and a phenomenon (the effect). Anything that affects an effect is a factor of that effect.
Confounding	In statistics, a confounding variable (also confounding factor, hidden variable, lurking variable, a confound, or confounder) is an extraneous variable in a statistical model that correlates (positively or negatively) with both the dependent variable and the independent variable. Such a relation between two observed variables is termed a spurious relationship. In the case of risk assessments evaluating the magnitude and nature of risk to human health, it is important to control for confounding to isolate the effect of a particular hazard such as a food additive, pesticide, or new drug.
Hypothetico-deductive model	The hypothetico-deductive model, first so-named by William Whewell, is a proposed description of scientific method. According to it, scientific inquiry proceeds by formulating a hypothesis in a form that could conceivably be falsified by a test on observable data. A test that could and does run contrary to predictions of the hypothesis is taken as a falsification of the hypothesis.
Variation	A Variation can refer to a specific sequence of successive moves in a turn-based game, often used to specify a hypothetical future state of a game that is being played. Although the term is most commonly used in the context of Chess analysis, it has been applied to other games. It also is a useful term used when describing computer tree-search algorithms (for example minimax) for playing games such as Go or Chess.

Chapter 1. Why is my evil lecturer forcing me to learn statistics?

17

Bonferroni correction	In statistics, the Bonferroni correction is a method used to counteract the problem of multiple comparisons. It is considered the simplest and most conservative method to control the familywise error rate. Informal introduction

Statistical inference logic is based on rejecting the null hypotheses if the likelihood under the null hypotheses of the observed data is low. |
| Precision | In statistics, the term precision can mean a quantity defined in a specific way. This is in addition to its more general meaning in the contexts of accuracy and precision and of precision and recall.

There can be differences in usage of the term for particular statistical models but, in general statistical usage, the precision is defined to be the reciprocal of the variance, while the precision matrix is the matrix inverse of the covariance matrix. |
| Practice effect | Practice effect is a systematic change (increase or decrease) in performance over a series of treatment conditions in a repeated measures (within-subjects) designt. A potential source of error usually neutralized by using a counterbalancing design. |
| Randomization | Randomization is the process of making something random; this means:•Generating a random permutation of a sequence (such as when shuffling cards)•Selecting a random sample of a population (important in statistical sampling)•Allocating experimental units via random assignment to a treatment or control condition•Generating random numbers•Transforming a data stream (such as when using a scrambler in telecommunications)

Randomization is not haphazard. Instead, a random process is a sequence of random variables describing a process whose outcomes do not follow a deterministic pattern, but follow an evolution described by probability distributions. For example, a random sample of individuals from a population refers to a sample where every individual has a known probability of being sampled. |
| Frequency distribution | In statistics, a frequency distribution is an arrangement of the values that one or more variables take in a sample. Each entry in the table contains the frequency or count of the occurrences of values within a particular group or interval, and in this way, the table summarizes the distribution of values in the sample. Univariate frequency tables

A different tabulation scheme aggregates values into bins such that each bin encompasses a range of values. |
| Histogram | In statistics, a histogram is a graphical representation showing a visual impression of the distribution of data. |

Chapter 1. Why is my evil lecturer forcing me to learn statistics?

It is an estimate of the probability distribution of a continuous variable and was first introduced by Karl Pearson. A histogram consists of tabular frequencies, shown as adjacent rectangles, erected over discrete intervals (bins), with an area equal to the frequency of the observations in the interval.

Logistic regression

In statistics, logistic regression is a type of regression analysis used for predicting the outcome of a categorical (a variable that can take on a limited number of categories) dependent variable based on one or more predictor variables. The probabilities describing the possible outcome of a single trial are modelled, as a function of explanatory variables, using a logistic function.

Logistic regression measures the relationship between a categorical dependent variable and usually a continuous independent variable, by converting the dependent variable to probability scores.

Normal distribution

In probability theory, the normal distribution is a continuous probability distribution that has a bell-shaped probability density function, known as the Gaussian function or informally the bell curve:

$$f(x; \mu, \sigma^2) = \frac{1}{\sigma\sqrt{2\pi}} e^{-\frac{1}{2}\left(\frac{x-\mu}{\sigma}\right)^2}$$

The parameter μ is the mean or expectation (location of the peak) and σ^2 is the variance. σ is known as the standard deviation. The distribution with $\mu = 0$ and $\sigma^2 = 1$ is called the standard normal distribution or the unit normal distribution.

Kurtosis

In probability theory and statistics, kurtosis is any measure of the 'peakedness' of the probability distribution of a real-valued random variable. In a similar way to the concept of skewness, kurtosis is a descriptor of the shape of a probability distribution and, just as for skewness, there are different ways of quantifying it for a theoretical distribution and corresponding ways of estimating it from a sample from a population. There are various interpretations of kurtosis, and of how particular measures should be interpreted; these are primarily peakedness (width of peak), tail weight, and lack of shoulders (distribution primarily peak and tails, not in between).

Negative skew

In probability theory and statistics, skewness is a measure of the asymmetry of the probability distribution of a real-valued random variable.

Consider the distribution on the figure. The bars on the right side of the distribution taper differently than the bars on the left side. These tapering sides are called tails, and they provide a visual means for determining which of the two kinds of skewness a distribution has:

· negative skew: The left tail is longer; the mass of the distribution is concentrated on the right of the figure.

Chapter 1. Why is my evil lecturer forcing me to learn statistics?

19

Platykurtic distribution	A distribution with negative kurtosis is called platykurtic. In terms of shape, a platykurtic distribution has a smaller 'peak' around the mean (that is, a lower probability than a normally distributed variable of values near the mean) and 'thin tails' (that is, a lower probability than a normally distributed variable of extreme values).
Positive skew	In probability theory and statistics, skewness is a measure of the asymmetry of the probability distribution of a real-valued random variable. The skewness value can be positive or negative, or even undefined. Qualitatively, a negative skew indicates that the tail on the left side of the probability density function is longer than the right side and the bulk of the values (including the median) lie to the right of the mean. A Positive skew indicates that the tail on the right side is longer than the left side and the bulk of the values lie to the left of the mean. A zero value indicates that the values are relatively evenly distributed on both sides of the mean, typically but not necessarily implying a symmetric distribution.
Sphericity	Sphericity is a measure of how spherical (round) an object is. As such, it is a specific example of a compactness measure of a shape. Defined by Wadell in 1935, the sphericity, Ψ, of a particle is: the ratio of the surface area of a sphere (with the same volume as the given particle) to the surface area of the particle: $$\Psi = \frac{\pi^{\frac{1}{3}}(6V_p)^{\frac{2}{3}}}{A_p}$$ where V_p is volume of the particle and A_p is the surface area of the particle.
Bimodal distribution	In statistics, a bimodal distribution is a continuous probability distribution with two different modes. These appear as distinct peaks (local maxima) in the probability density function. Terminology When the two modes are unequal the larger mode is known as the major mode and the other as the minor mode.
Central tendency	In statistics, the term central tendency relates to the way in which quantitative data tend to cluster around some value. A measure of central tendency is any of a number of ways of specifying this 'central value'. In practical statistical analysis, the terms are often used before one has chosen even a preliminary form of analysis: thus an initial objective might be to 'choose an appropriate measure of central tendency'.
Centre	In geometry, the centre of an object is a point in some sense in the middle of the object. If geometry is regarded as the study of isometry groups then the centre is a fixed point of the isometries.

Chapter 1. Why is my evil lecturer forcing me to learn statistics?

Mode	The mode is the number that appears most often in a set of numbers.
	Like the statistical mean and median, the mode is a way of capturing important information about a random variable or a population in a single quantity. The mode is in general different from the mean and median, and may be very different for strongly skewed distributions.
Median	In probability theory and statistics, a median is described as the numerical value separating the higher half of a sample, a population, or a probability distribution, from the lower half. The median of a finite list of numbers can be found by arranging all the observations from lowest value to highest value and picking the middle one. If there is an even number of observations, then there is no single middle value; the median is then usually defined to be the mean of the two middle values.
Multimodal distribution	In statistics, a bimodal distribution is a continuous probability distribution with two different modes. These appear as distinct peaks (local maxima) in the probability density function.
	More generally, a multimodal distribution is a continuous probability distribution with two or more modes.
Distribution	In differential geometry, a discipline within mathematics, a distribution is a subset of the tangent bundle of a manifold satisfying certain properties.
Interquartile range	In descriptive statistics, the interquartile range also called the midspread or middle fifty, is a measure of statistical dispersion, being equal to the difference between the upper and lower quartiles, IQR = $Q_3 - Q_1$ Use
	Unlike (total) range, the interquartile range has a breakdown point of 25%, and is thus often preferred to the total range.
	The IQR is used to build box plots, simple graphical representations of a probability distribution.
	For a symmetric distribution (where the median equals the midhinge, the average of the first and third quartiles), half the IQR equals the median absolute deviation (MAD).
Lower quartile	In descriptive statistics, a quartile is any of the three values which divide the sorted data set into four equal parts, so that each part represents one fourth of the sampled population.
	In epidemiology, the quartiles are the four ranges defined by the three values discussed here.
	· first quartile (designated Q_1) = Lower quartile = cuts off lowest 25% of data = 25th percentile · second quartile (designated Q_2) = median = cuts data set in half = 50th percentile

Chapter 1. Why is my evil lecturer forcing me to learn statistics?

21

CHAPTER HIGHLIGHTS & NOTES: KEY TERMS, PEOPLE, PLACES, CONCEPTS

· third quartile (designated Q_3) = upper quartile = cuts off highest 25% of data, or lowest 75% = 75th percentile

The difference between the upper and Lower quartiles(n)left(cfrac{y}{100} ight).' src='../../tx/pod/38e9246c395ff4800c290c59a6fcd09c.png'>

· Case 1: If L is a whole number, then the value will be found halfway between positions L and L+1.
· Case 2: If L is a decimal, round up to the nearest whole number. (for example, L = 1.2 becomes 2).

Method 1

· Use the median to divide the ordered data set into two halves.

Quartile	In descriptive statistics, the quartiles of a set of values are the three points that divide the data set into four equal groups, each representing a fourth of the population being sampled. A quartile is a type of quantile. In epidemiology, sociology and finance, the quartiles of a population are the four subpopulations defined by classifying individuals according to whether the value concerned falls into one of the four ranges defined by the three values discussed above.
Second quartile	lower quartile and upper quartile In descriptive statistics, a quartile is any of the three values which divide the sorted data set into four equal parts, so that each part represents one fourth of the sampled population. In epidemiology, the quartiles are the four ranges defined by the three values discussed here. · first quartile (designated Q_1) = lower quartile = cuts off lowest 25% of data = 25th percentile · second quartile = median = cuts data set in half = 50th percentile · third quartile (designated Q_3) = upper quartile = cuts off highest 25% of data, or lowest 75% = 75th percentile The difference between the upper and lower quartiles is called the interquartile range. There is no universal agreement on choosing the quartile values. The formula for locating the position of the observation at a given percentile, y, with n data points sorted in ascending order is:

Chapter 1. Why is my evil lecturer forcing me to learn statistics?

CHAPTER HIGHLIGHTS & NOTES: KEY TERMS, PEOPLE, PLACES, CONCEPTS

· Case 1: If L is a whole number, then the value will be found halfway between positions L and L+1.

· Case 2: If L is a decimal, round up to the nearest whole number.

Third quartile	The third quartile is designated as Q_3. The upper quartile cuts off highest 25% of data or lowest 75%.
Deviance	In statistics, deviance is a quality of fit statistic for a model that is often used for statistical hypothesis testing. The deviance for a model M_0, based on a dataset y, is defined as $$D(y) = -2\Big(\log\left(p(y|\hat{\theta}_0)\right) - \log\left(p(y|\hat{\theta}_s)\right) \Big).$$ Here $\hat{\theta}_0$ denotes the fitted values of the parameters in the model M_0, while $\hat{\theta}_s$ denotes the fitted parameters for the 'full model' : both sets of fitted values are implicitly functions of the observations y. Here the full model is a model with a parameter for every observation so that the data are fitted exactly.
Percentile	In statistics and the social sciences, a percentile is the value of a variable below which a certain percent of observations fall. For example, the 20th percentile is the value (or score) below which 20 percent of the observations may be found. The term percentile and the related term percentile rank are often used in the reporting of scores from norm-referenced tests.
Quantile	Quantiles are points taken at regular intervals from the cumulative distribution function (CDF) of a random variable. Dividing ordered data into q essentially equal-sized data subsets is the motivation for q-quantiles; the quantiles are the data values marking the boundaries between consecutive subsets. Put another way, the kth q-quantile for a random variable is the value x such that the probability that the random variable will be less than x is at most k/q and the probability that the random variable will be more than x is at most $$(q-k)/q = 1 - (k/q).$$
Deviation	In mathematics and statistics, deviation is a measure of difference between the observed value and the mean. The sign of deviation (positive or negative), reports the direction of that difference (it is larger when the sign is positive, and smaller if it is negative). The magnitude of the value indicates the size of the difference.
Variance	In probability theory and statistics, the variance is a measure of how far a set of numbers is spread out. It is one of several descriptors of a probability distribution, describing how far the numbers lie from the mean (expected value).

Chapter 1. Why is my evil lecturer forcing me to learn statistics?

23

Standard deviation	In statistics and probability theory, standard deviation shows how much variation or 'dispersion' exists from the average (mean, or expected value). A low standard deviation indicates that the data points tend to be very close to the mean; high standard deviation indicates that the data points are spread out over a large range of values.
	The standard deviation of a random variable, statistical population, data set, or probability distribution is the square root of its variance.
Probability distribution	In probability and statistics, a probability distribution assigns a probability to each of the possible outcomes of a random experiment. Examples are found in experiments whose sample space is non-numerical, where the distribution would be a categorical distribution; experiments whose sample space is encoded by discrete random variables, where the distribution is a probability mass function; and experiments with sample spaces encoded by continuous random variables, where the distribution is a probability density function. More complex experiments, such as those involving stochastic processes defined in continuous-time, may demand the use of more general probability measures.
Density function	In probability theory, a probability density function or density of a continuous random variable, is a function that describes the relative likelihood for this random variable to take on a given value. The probability for the random variable to fall within a particular region is given by the integral of this variable's density over the region. The probability density function is nonnegative everywhere, and its integral over the entire space is equal to one.
Probability density function	In probability theory, a probability density function or density of a continuous random variable, is a function that describes the relative likelihood for this random variable to take on a given value. The probability for the random variable to fall within a particular region is given by the integral of this variable's density over the region. The probability density function is nonnegative everywhere, and its integral over the entire space is equal to one.
Statistical model	A statistical model is a formalization of relationships between variables in the form of mathematical equations. A statistical model describes how one or more random variables are related to one or more other variables. The model is statistical as the variables are not deterministically but stochastically related.
Standard error	The standard error is the standard deviation of the sampling distribution of a statistic. The term may also be used to refer to an estimate of that standard deviation, derived from a particular sample used to compute the estimate.
	For example, the sample mean is the usual estimator of a population mean.
Presentation Layer	The Presentation Layer is Layer 6 of the seven-layer OSI model of computer networking.

Chapter 1. Why is my evil lecturer forcing me to learn statistics?

The Presentation Layer is responsible for the delivery and formatting of information to the application layer for further processing or display. It relieves the application layer of concern regarding syntactical differences in data representation within the end-user systems.

Wright

In software architecture, Wright is an architecture description language developed at Carnegie Mellon University. Wright formalizes a software architecture in terms of concepts such as components, connectors, roles, and ports. The dynamic behavior of different ports of an individual component is described using the Communicating Sequential Processes (CSP) process algebra.

1. The _____ is the number that appears most often in a set of numbers.

    Like the statistical mean and median, the _____ is a way of capturing important information about a random variable or a population in a single quantity. The _____ is in general different from the mean and median, and may be very different for strongly skewed distributions.

    a. Pareto index
    b. Mode
    c. Confocal
    d. Conway polyhedron notation

2. _____ Statistics is a software package used for statistical analysis. It is now officially named 'IBM _____ Statistics'. Companion products in the same family are used for survey authoring and deployment (IBM _____ Data Collection), data mining (IBM _____ Modeler), text analytics, and collaboration and deployment (batch and automated scoring services).

    a. StatCVS
    b. Statgraphics
    c. Statistical Solutions
    d. SPSS

3. . In statistics and data analysis, a _____ is an original datum that has not been transformed. This may include, for example, the original result obtained by a student on a test (i.e., the number of correctly answered items) as opposed to that score after transformation to a standard score or percentile rank or the like.

    Often the conversion must be made to a standard score before the data can be used.

Chapter 1. Why is my evil lecturer forcing me to learn statistics?

25

CHAPTER QUIZ: KEY TERMS, PEOPLE, PLACES, CONCEPTS

   a. Realization
   b. Standard error
   c. Raw score
   d. Ridge regression

4. The _____ is designated as Q_3. The upper quartile cuts off highest 25% of data or lowest 75%.

   a. Sphericity
   b. Relative-frequency distribution
   c. Class frequency
   d. Third quartile

5. In statistical hypothesis testing, a hypothesis test is typically specified in terms of a _____, which is a function of the sample; it is considered as a numerical summary of a set of data that reduces the data to one or a small number of values that can be used to perform a hypothesis test. Given a null hypothesis and a _____ T, we can specify a 'null value' T_0 such that values of T close to T_0 present the strongest evidence in favor of the null hypothesis, whereas values of T far from T_0 present the strongest evidence against the null hypothesis. An important property of a

   _____ is that we must be able to determine its sampling distribution under the null hypothesis, which allows us to calculate p-values.

   a. Time-varying covariate
   b. Power transform
   c. Test statistic
   d. Ceiling effect

1. b
2. d
3. c
4. d
5. c

You can take the complete Chapter Practice Test

for Chapter 1. Why is my evil lecturer forcing me to learn statistics?
on all key terms, persons, places, and concepts.

Online 99 Cents

http://www.epub27.31.21776.1.cram101.com/

Use www.Cram101.com for all your study needs

including Cram101's online interactive problem solving labs in

chemistry, statistics, mathematics, and more.

Chapter 2. Everything you never wanted to know about statistics

_____ Statistical model

_____ Factor analysis

_____ Linear model

_____ Parameter

_____ Sampling

_____ Degree

_____ Degrees of freedom

_____ Freedom

_____ Least squares

_____ Hypothetico-deductive model

_____ Sample mean

_____ Sampling distribution

_____ Central limit theorem

_____ Confidence interval

_____ Interval

_____ Student t distribution

_____ Null hypothesis

_____ Hypothesis

_____ Randomization

CHAPTER OUTLINE: KEY TERMS, PEOPLE, PLACES, CONCEPTS

Ronald Aylmer Fisher

Test statistic

Variation

One- and two-tailed tests

Two-tailed test

Levene's test

Experimentwise error rate

Familywise error rate

Bonferroni correction

Carlo Emilio Bonferroni

Statistical power

Sample size

Statistical significance

English

Categorical data

Effect size

Meta-analysis

Chapter 2. Everything you never wanted to know about statistics

Statistical model	A statistical model is a formalization of relationships between variables in the form of mathematical equations. A statistical model describes how one or more random variables are related to one or more other variables. The model is statistical as the variables are not deterministically but stochastically related.
Factor analysis	Factor analysis is a statistical method used to describe variability among observed, correlated variables in terms of a potentially lower number of unobserved variables called factors. In other words, it is possible, for example, that variations in three or four observed variables mainly reflect the variations in fewer unobserved variables. Factor analysis searches for such joint variations in response to unobserved latent variables.
Linear model	In statistics, the term linear model is used in different ways according to the context. The most common occurrence is in connection with regression models and the term is often taken as synonymous with linear regression model. However, the term is also used in time series analysis with a different meaning.
Parameter	Parameter can be interpreted in mathematics, logic, linguistics, environmental science and other disciplines. In its common meaning, the term is used to identify a characteristic, a feature, a measurable factor that can help in defining a particular system. It is an important element to take into consideration for the evaluation or for the comprehension of an event, a project or any situation.
Sampling	In statistics and survey methodology, sampling is concerned with the selection of a subset of individuals from within a population to estimate characteristics of the whole population. Researchers rarely survey the entire population because the cost of a census is too high. The three main advantages of sampling are that the cost is lower, data collection is faster, and since the data set is smaller it is possible to ensure homogeneity and to improve the accuracy and quality of the data.
Degree	In mathematics, there are several meanings of degree depending on the subject. A degree (in full, a degree of arc, arc degree, or arcdegree), usually denoted by ° (the degree symbol), is a measurement of a plane angle, representing $\frac{1}{360}$ of a turn. When that angle is with respect to a reference meridian, it indicates a location along a great circle of a sphere, such as Earth , Mars, or the celestial sphere.
Degrees of freedom	In statistics, the number of degrees of freedom is the number of values in the final calculation of a statistic that are free to vary.

	Estimates of statistical parameters can be based upon different amounts of information or data. The number of independent pieces of information that go into the estimate of a parameter is called the degrees of freedom (df).
Freedom	Freedom (often referred to as the Freedom app) is a software program designed to keep a computer user away from the Internet for up to eight hours at a time. It is described as a way to 'free you from distractions, allowing you time to write, analyze, code, or create.' The program was written by Fred Stutzman, a Ph.D student at the University of North Carolina at Chapel Hill. Freedom is donationware.
Least squares	In mathematics, the idea of least squares can be applied to approximating a given function by a weighted sum of other functions. The best approximation can be defined as that which minimises the difference between the original function and the approximation; for a least-squares approach the quality of the approximation is measured in terms of the squared differences the two. Functional analysis

A generalization to approximation of a data set is the approximation of a function by a sum of other functions, usually an orthogonal set: $$f(x) \approx f_n(x) = a_1\phi_1(x) + a_2\phi_2(x) + \cdots + a_n\phi_n(x),$$ with the set of functions { $\phi_j(x)$ } an orthonormal set over the interval of interest, say [a, b]. |
Hypothetico-deductive model	The hypothetico-deductive model, first so-named by William Whewell, is a proposed description of scientific method. According to it, scientific inquiry proceeds by formulating a hypothesis in a form that could conceivably be falsified by a test on observable data. A test that could and does run contrary to predictions of the hypothesis is taken as a falsification of the hypothesis.
Sample mean	The sample mean or empirical mean and the sample covariance are statistics computed from a collection of data on one or more random variables. The sample mean is a vector each of whose elements is the sample mean of one of the random variables - that is, each of whose elements is the average of the observed values of one of the variables. The sample covariance is a square matrix whose i, j element is the covariance between the sets of observed values of two of the variables and whose i, i element is the variance of the observed values of one of the variables.
Sampling distribution	In statistics, a sampling distribution is the probability distribution of a given statistic based on a random sample. Sampling distributions are important in statistics because they provide a major simplification on the route to statistical inference.

Chapter 2. Everything you never wanted to know about statistics

Central limit theorem	In probability theory, the central limit theorem states that, given certain conditions, the mean of a sufficiently large number of independent random variables, each with finite mean and variance, will be approximately normally distributed. The central limit theorem has a number of variants. In its common form, the random variables must be identically distributed.
Confidence interval	In statistics, a confidence interval is a type of interval estimate of a population parameter and is used to indicate the reliability of an estimate. It is an observed interval (i.e. it is calculated from the observations), in principle different from sample to sample, that frequently includes the parameter of interest if the experiment is repeated. How frequently the observed interval contains the parameter is determined by the confidence level or confidence coefficient.
Interval	In mathematics, a (real) interval is a set of real numbers with the property that any number that lies between two numbers in the set is also included in the set. For example, the set of all numbers x satisfying $0 \le x \le 1$ is an interval which contains 0 and 1, as well as all numbers between them. Other examples of intervals are the set of all real numbers $\mathbb{R}$, the set of all negative real numbers, and the empty set.
Student t distribution	The Student t distribution is a probability distribution that arises in the problem of estimating the mean of a normally distributed population when the sample size is small. It is the basis of the popular Student's t-tests for the statistical significance of the difference between two sample means, and for confidence intervals for the difference between two population means.
Null hypothesis	The practice of science involves formulating and testing hypotheses, statements that are capable of being proven false using a test of observed data. The null hypothesis typically corresponds to a general or default position. For example, the null hypothesis might be that there is no relationship between two measured phenomena or that a potential treatment has no effect.
Hypothesis	A hypothesis is a proposed explanation for a phenomenon. For a hypothesis to be a scientific hypothesis, the scientific method requires that one can test it. Scientists generally base scientific hypotheses on previous observations that cannot satisfactorily be explained with the available scientific theories.
Randomization	Randomization is the process of making something random; this means:•Generating a random permutation of a sequence (such as when shuffling cards)•Selecting a random sample of a population (important in statistical sampling)•Allocating experimental units via random assignment to a treatment or control condition•Generating random numbers•Transforming a data stream (such as when using a scrambler in telecommunications) Randomization is not haphazard.

Instead, a random process is a sequence of random variables describing a process whose outcomes do not follow a deterministic pattern, but follow an evolution described by probability distributions. For example, a random sample of individuals from a population refers to a sample where every individual has a known probability of being sampled.

Ronald Aylmer Fisher	Sir Ronald Aylmer Fisher FRS (17 February 1890 - 29 July 1962) was an English statistician, evolutionary biologist, eugenicist and geneticist. He was described by Anders Hald as 'a genius who almost single-handedly created the foundations for modern statistical science,' and Richard Dawkins described him as 'the greatest of Darwin's successors'.
Test statistic	In statistical hypothesis testing, a hypothesis test is typically specified in terms of a test statistic, which is a function of the sample; it is considered as a numerical summary of a set of data that reduces the data to one or a small number of values that can be used to perform a hypothesis test. Given a null hypothesis and a test statistic T, we can specify a 'null value' T_0 such that values of T close to T_0 present the strongest evidence in favor of the null hypothesis, whereas values of T far from T_0 present the strongest evidence against the null hypothesis. An important property of a test statistic is that we must be able to determine its sampling distribution under the null hypothesis, which allows us to calculate p-values.
Variation	A Variation can refer to a specific sequence of successive moves in a turn-based game, often used to specify a hypothetical future state of a game that is being played. Although the term is most commonly used in the context of Chess analysis, it has been applied to other games. It also is a useful term used when describing computer tree-search algorithms (for example minimax) for playing games such as Go or Chess.
One- and two-tailed tests	The two-tailed test is a statistical test used in inference, in which a given statistical hypothesis, H_0 (the null hypothesis), will be rejected when the value of the test statistic is either sufficiently small or sufficiently large. This contrasts with a one-tailed test, in which only one of the rejection regions 'sufficiently small' or 'sufficiently large' is preselected according to the alternative hypothesis being selected, and the hypothesis is rejected only if the test statistic satisfies that criterion. Alternative names are one-sided and two-sided tests. However, the terminology is extended to tests relating to distributions other than normal. In general a test is called two-tailed if the null hypothesis is rejected for values of the test statistic falling into either tail of its sampling distribution, and it is called one-sided or one-tailed if the null hypothesis is rejected only for values of the test statistic falling into one specified tail of its sampling distribution. For example, if the alternative hypothesis is $\mu \neq 42.5$, rejecting the null hypothesis of $\mu = 42.5$ for small or for large values of the sample mean, the test is called 'two-tailed' or 'two-sided'. If the alternative hypothesis is $\mu > 1.4$, rejecting the null hypothesis of

$\mu \leq 1.4$ only for large values of the sample mean, it is then called 'one-tailed' or 'one-sided'.

If the distribution from which the samples are derived is considered to be normal, Gaussian, or bell-shaped, then the test is referred to as a one- or two-tailed T test. If the test is performed using the actual population mean and variance, rather than an estimate from a sample, it would be called a one- or two-tailed Z test.

The statistical tables for Z and for t provide critical values for both one- and two-tailed tests.

Two-tailed test	The two-tailed test is a statistical test used in inference, in which a given statistical hypothesis, H_0 (the null hypothesis), will be rejected when the value of the test statistic is either sufficiently small or sufficiently large. This contrasts with a one-tailed test, in which only one of the rejection regions 'sufficiently small' or 'sufficiently large' is preselected according to the alternative hypothesis being selected, and the hypothesis is rejected only if the test statistic satisfies that criterion. Alternative names are one-sided and two-sided tests. However, the terminology is extended to tests relating to distributions other than normal. In general a test is called two-tailed if the null hypothesis is rejected for values of the test statistic falling into either tail of its sampling distribution, and it is called one-sided or one-tailed if the null hypothesis is rejected only for values of the test statistic falling into one specified tail of its sampling distribution. For example, if the alternative hypothesis is $\mu \neq 42.5$, rejecting the null hypothesis of μ = 42.5 for small or for large values of the sample mean, the test is called 'two-tailed' or 'two-sided'. If the alternative hypothesis is μ > 1.4, rejecting the null hypothesis of $\mu \leq 1.4$ only for large values of the sample mean, it is then called 'one-tailed' or 'one-sided'. If the distribution from which the samples are derived is considered to be normal, Gaussian, or bell-shaped, then the test is referred to as a one- or two-tailed T test. If the test is performed using the actual population mean and variance, rather than an estimate from a sample, it would be called a one- or two-tailed Z test.
Levene's test	In statistics, Levene's test is an inferential statistic used to assess the equality of variances in different samples. Some common statistical procedures assume that variances of the populations from which different samples are drawn are equal. Levene's test assesses this assumption.
Experimentwise error rate	In statistics, during multiple comparisons testing, experimentwise error rate is the probability of at least one false rejection of the null hypothesis over an entire experiment. The α (alpha) that is assigned applies to all of the hypothesis tests as a whole, not individually as in the comparisonwise error rate.

Familywise error rate	In statistics, familywise error rate is the probability of making one or more false discoveries, or type I errors among all the hypotheses when performing multiple hypotheses tests. FWER definition
	Suppose we have m null hypotheses, denoted by: H_1, H_2, .. H_m. Using a statistical test, each hypothesis is declared significant/non-significant. Summing the test results over H_i will give us the following table and related random variables:• m_0 is the number of true null hypotheses, an unknown parameter• $m - m_0$ is the number of true alternative hypotheses• V is the number of false positives (Type I error)• S is the number of true positives• T is the number of false negatives (Type II error)• U is the number of true negatives• R is the number of rejected null hypotheses• R is an observable random variable, while S, T, U, and V are unobservable random variables
	The FWER is the probability of making even one type I error In the family, $$\text{FWER} = \Pr(V \geq 1),$$ or equivalently, $$\text{FWER} = 1 - \Pr(V = 0).$$ Thus, by assuring $\text{FWER} \leq \alpha,$, the probability of making even one type I error in the family is controlled at level α
	A procedure controls the FWER in the weak sense if the FWER control at level α is guaranteed only when all null hypotheses are true (i.e. when $m_0 = m$ so the global null hypothesis is true)
	A procedure controls the FWER in the strong sense if the FWER control at level α is guaranteed for any configuration of true and non-true null hypotheses (including the global null hypothesis) The concept of a family
	Within the statistical framework, there are several definitions for the term 'family':•First of all, a distinction must be made between exploratory data analysis and confirmatory data analysis: for exploratory analysis - the family constitutes all inferences made and those that potentially could be made, whereas in the case of confirmatory analysis, the family must include only inferences of interest specified prior to the study•Hochberg & Tamhane (1987) define 'family' as 'any collection of inferences for which it is meaningful to take into account some combined measure of error'•According to Cox (1982), a set of inferences should be regarded a family:•To take into account the selection effect due to data dredging•To ensure simultaneous correctness of a set of inferences as to guarantee a correct overall decision

Chapter 2. Everything you never wanted to know about statistics

To summarize, a family could best be defined by the potential selective inference that is being faced: A family is the smallest set of items of inference in an analysis, interchangeable about their meaning for the goal of research, from which selection of results for action, presentation or highlighting could be made (Benjamini).

Tukey first coined the term experimentwise error rate and 'per-experiment' error rate for the error rate that the researcher should use as a control level in a multiple hypothesis experiment.

Bonferroni correction	In statistics, the Bonferroni correction is a method used to counteract the problem of multiple comparisons. It is considered the simplest and most conservative method to control the familywise error rate. Informal introduction
	Statistical inference logic is based on rejecting the null hypotheses if the likelihood under the null hypotheses of the observed data is low.
Carlo Emilio Bonferroni	Carlo Emilio Bonferroni was an Italian mathematician who worked on probability theory. Carlo Emilio Bonferroni was born in Bergamo on 28 January 1892 and died on 18 August 1960 in Firenze (Florence). He studied in Torino (Turin), held a post as assistant professor at the Turin Polytechnic, and in 1923 took up the chair of financial mathematics at the Economics Institute in Bari.
Statistical power	The power of a statistical test is the probability that the test will reject the null hypothesis when the null hypothesis is actually false (i.e. the probability of not committing a Type II error, or making a false negative decision). The power is in general a function of the possible distributions, often determined by a parameter, under the alternative hypothesis. As the power increases, the chances of a Type II error occurring decrease. The probability of a Type II error occurring is referred to as the false negative rate (β). Therefore power is equal to $1 - \beta$, which is also known as the sensitivity.
	Power analysis can be used to calculate the minimum sample size required so that one can be reasonably likely to detect an effect of a given size. Power analysis can also be used to calculate the minimum effect size that is likely to be detected in a study using a given sample size. In addition, the concept of power is used to make comparisons between different statistical testing procedures: for example, between a parametric and a nonparametric test of the same hypothesis. Background
	Statistical tests use data from samples to assess, or make inferences about, a population. In the concrete setting of a two-sample comparison, the goal is to assess whether the mean values of some attribute obtained for individuals in two sub-populations differ.

For example, to test the null hypothesis that the mean scores of men and women on a test do not differ, samples of men and women are drawn, the test is administered to them, and the mean score of one group is compared to that of the other group using a statistical test such as the two-sample z-test. The power of the test is the probability that the test will find a statistically significant difference between men and women, as a function of the size of the true difference between those two populations. Note that power is the probability of finding a difference that does exist, as opposed to the likelihood of declaring a difference that does not exist (which is known as a Type I error, or 'false positive'). Factors influencing power

Statistical power may depend on a number of factors.

Sample size	Sample size determination is the act of choosing the number of observations or replicates to include in a statistical sample. The sample size is an important feature of any empirical study in which the goal is to make inferences about a population from a sample. In practice, the sample size used in a study is determined based on the expense of data collection, and the need to have sufficient statistical power.
Statistical significance	Statistical significance is a statistical assessment of whether observations reflect a pattern rather than just chance. The fundamental challenge is that any partial picture of a given hypothesis, poll or question is subject to random error. In statistical testing, a result is deemed statistically significant if it is so extreme (without external variables which would influence the correlation results of the test) that such a result would be expected to arise simply by chance only in rare circumstances.
English	English is a database retrieval and reporting language somewhat like SQL, but with no programming or update abilities. It was originally released by Microdata in 1973 and named so that the company's brochures could claim that developers could generate reports on their implementation of the Pick operating system using English.
Categorical data	In statistics, categorical data is that part of an observed dataset that consists of categorical variables, or for data that has been converted into that form, for example as grouped data. More specifically, categorical data may derive from either or both of observations made of qualitative data, where the observations are summarised as counts or cross tabulations, or of quantitative data, where observations might be directly observed counts of events happening or they might counts of values that occur within given intervals. Often, purely categorical data are summarised in the form of a contingency table.
Effect size	In statistics, an effect size is a measure of the strength of a phenomenon (for example, the relationship between two variables in a statistical population) or a sample-based estimate of that quantity.

Chapter 2. Everything you never wanted to know about statistics

	An effect size calculated from data is a descriptive statistic that conveys the estimated magnitude of a relationship without making any statement about whether the apparent relationship in the data reflects a true relationship in the population. In that way, effect sizes complement inferential statistics such as p-values.
Meta-analysis	In statistics, a meta-analysis refers to methods focused on contrasting and combining results from different studies, in the hope of identifying patterns among study results, sources of disagreement among those results, or other interesting relationships that may come to light in the context of multiple studies. In its simplest form, this is normally by identification of a common measure of effect size, of which a weighted average might be the output of a meta-analysis. The weighting might be related to sample sizes within the individual studies.

1. The _____, first so-named by William Whewell, is a proposed description of scientific method. According to it, scientific inquiry proceeds by formulating a hypothesis in a form that could conceivably be falsified by a test on observable data. A test that could and does run contrary to predictions of the hypothesis is taken as a falsification of the hypothesis.

   a. Jadad scale
   b. Mature technology
   c. Hypothetico-deductive model
   d. Multiple discovery

2. In mathematics, there are several meanings of _____ depending on the subject.

   A _____ (in full, a _____ of arc, arc _____, or arc_____), usually denoted by ° (the _____ symbol), is a measurement of a plane angle, representing $\frac{1}{360}$ of a turn. When that angle is with respect to a reference meridian, it indicates a location along a great circle of a sphere, such as Earth , Mars, or the celestial sphere.

   a. Discharging method
   b. Degree
   c. Frequency partition of a graph
   d. Graph

3. . In statistics, a _____ is a type of interval estimate of a population parameter and is used to indicate the reliability of an estimate. It is an observed interval (i.e. it is calculated from the observations), in principle different from sample to sample, that frequently includes the parameter of interest if the experiment is repeated. How frequently the observed interval contains the parameter is determined by the confidence level or confidence coefficient.

a. Consensus forecast

b. Constant elasticity of substitution

c. Confidence interval

d. Diversification

4. . In statistics, _____ is the probability of making one or more false discoveries, or type I errors among all the hypotheses when performing multiple hypotheses tests. FWER definition

Suppose we have m null hypotheses, denoted by: H_1, H_2, .. H_m.Using a statistical test, each hypothesis is declared significant/non-significant.Summing the test results over H_i will give us the following table and related random variables:• m_0 is the number of true null hypotheses, an unknown parameter• $m - m_0$ is the number of true alternative hypotheses• V is the number of false positives (Type I error)• S is the number of true positives• T is the number of false negatives (Type II error)• U is the number of true negatives• R is the number of rejected null hypotheses• R is an observable random variable, while S, T, U, and V are unobservable random variables

The FWER is the probability of making even one type I error In the family, $\mathrm{FWER} = \mathrm{Pr}(V \geq 1),$

or equivalently, $\mathrm{FWER} = 1 - \mathrm{Pr}(V = 0).$

Thus, by assuring $\mathrm{FWER} \leq \alpha,$, the probability of making even one type I error in the family is controlled at level α

A procedure controls the FWER in the weak sense if the FWER control at level α is guaranteed only when all null hypotheses are true (i.e. when m_0 = m so the global null hypothesis is true)

A procedure controls the FWER in the strong sense if the FWER control at level α is guaranteed for any configuration of true and non-true null hypotheses (including the global null hypothesis) The concept of a family

Within the statistical framework, there are several definitions for the term 'family':•First of all, a distinction must be made between exploratory data analysis and confirmatory data analysis: for exploratory analysis - the family constitutes all inferences made and those that potentially could be made, whereas in the case of confirmatory analysis, the family must include only inferences of interest specified prior to the study•Hochberg & Tamhane (1987) define 'family' as 'any collection of inferences for which it is meaningful to take into account some combined measure of error'•According to Cox (1982), a set of inferences should be regarded a family:•To take into account the selection effect due to data dredging•To ensure simultaneous correctness of a set of inferences as to guarantee a correct overall decision

To summarize, a family could best be defined by the potential selective inference that is being faced: A family is the smallest set of items of inference in an analysis, interchangeable about their meaning for the goal of research, from which selection of results for action, presentation or highlighting could be made (Benjamini).

Tukey first coined the term experimentwise error rate and 'per-experiment' error rate for the error rate that the researcher should use as a control level in a multiple hypothesis experiment.

a. Generalized p-value
b. Paired difference test
c. Per-comparison error rate
d. Familywise error rate

5. In statistical hypothesis testing, a hypothesis test is typically specified in terms of a _____, which is a function of the sample; it is considered as a numerical summary of a set of data that reduces the data to one or a small number of values that can be used to perform a hypothesis test. Given a null hypothesis and a _____ T, we can specify a 'null value' T_0 such that values of T close to T_0 present the strongest evidence in favor of the null hypothesis, whereas values of T far from T_0 present the strongest evidence against the null hypothesis. An important property of a _____ is that we must be able to determine its sampling distribution under the null hypothesis, which allows us to calculate p-values.

a. Time-varying covariate
b. Power transform
c. Test statistic
d. Ceiling effect

1. c
2. b
3. c
4. d
5. c

You can take the complete Chapter Practice Test

for Chapter 2. Everything you never wanted to know about statistics
on all key terms, persons, places, and concepts.

Online 99 Cents

http://www.epub27.31.21776.2.cram101.com/

Use www.Cram101.com for all your study needs

including Cram101's online interactive problem solving labs in

chemistry, statistics, mathematics, and more.

CHAPTER OUTLINE: KEY TERMS, PEOPLE, PLACES, CONCEPTS

	Opening
	Descriptive statistic
	Dimension reduction
	General linear model
	Mixed model
	Regression
	Utility
	Confidence interval
	Interval
	SPSS
	Decimal numeral system
	Missing data

Chapter 3. The IBM SPSS Statistics environment

Opening	You may be looking for: · Chess Opening · Al-Fatiha, 'The Opening', first chapter of the Qur'an. · Opening bid, a term from contract bridge. · Grand Opening of a business or other institution. · Vernissage, the Opening of an art exhibition. · Opening, a morphological filtering operation used in image processing. · The Opening credits or title sequence of a TV show or film. · Opening statement, a beginning statement in a court case. '
Descriptive statistic	Descriptive statistics are used to describe the main features of a collection of data in quantitative terms. Descriptive statistics are distinguished from inferential statistics (or inductive statistics), in that Descriptive statistics aim to quantitatively summarize a data set, rather than being used to support inferential statements about the population that the data are thought to represent. Even when a data analysis draws its main conclusions using inductive statistical analysis, Descriptive statistics are generally presented along with more formal analyses.
Dimension reduction	In machine learning, dimension reduction is the process of reducing the number of random variables under consideration, and can be divided into feature selection and feature extraction. Feature selection Feature selection approaches try to find a subset of the original variables (also called features or attributes). Two strategies are filter (e.g. information gain) and wrapper (e.g. search guided by the accuracy) approaches.
General linear model	The general linear model is a statistical linear model. It may be written as $\mathbf{Y} = \mathbf{XB} + \mathbf{U}$, where Y is a matrix with series of multivariate measurements, X is a matrix that might be a design matrix, B is a matrix containing parameters that are usually to be estimated and U is a matrix containing errors or noise. The errors are usually assumed to follow a multivariate normal distribution.
Mixed model	A mixed model is a statistical model containing both fixed effects and random effects, that is mixed effects. These models are useful in a wide variety of disciplines in the physical, biological and social sciences. They are particularly useful in settings where repeated measurements are made on the same statistical units, or where measurements are made on clusters of related statistical units.
Regression	Regression in medicine is a characteristic of diseases to show lighter symptoms without completely disappearing. At a later point, symptoms may return. These symptoms are then called recidive.

Chapter 3. The IBM SPSS Statistics environment

Utility	In economics, utility is a measure of relative satisfaction. Given this measure, one may speak meaningfully of increasing or decreasing utility, and thereby explain economic behavior in terms of attempts to increase one's utility. Utility is often modeled to be affected by consumption of various goods and services, possession of wealth and spending of leisure time.
Confidence interval	In statistics, a confidence interval is a type of interval estimate of a population parameter and is used to indicate the reliability of an estimate. It is an observed interval (i.e. it is calculated from the observations), in principle different from sample to sample, that frequently includes the parameter of interest if the experiment is repeated. How frequently the observed interval contains the parameter is determined by the confidence level or confidence coefficient.
Interval	In mathematics, a (real) interval is a set of real numbers with the property that any number that lies between two numbers in the set is also included in the set. For example, the set of all numbers x satisfying $0 \leq x \leq 1$ is an interval which contains 0 and 1, as well as all numbers between them. Other examples of intervals are the set of all real numbers $\mathbb{R}$, the set of all negative real numbers, and the empty set.
SPSS	SPSS Statistics is a software package used for statistical analysis. It is now officially named 'IBM SPSS Statistics'. Companion products in the same family are used for survey authoring and deployment (IBM SPSS Data Collection), data mining (IBM SPSS Modeler), text analytics, and collaboration and deployment (batch and automated scoring services).
Decimal numeral system	The Decimal numeral system has ten as its base. It is the numerical base most widely used by modern civilizations. Decimal notation often refers to the base-10 positional notation such as the Hindu-Arabic numeral system, however it can also be used more generally to refer to non-positional systems such as Roman or Chinese numerals which are also based on powers of ten.
Missing data	In statistics, missing data, occur when no data value is stored for the variable in the current observation. Missing data are a common occurrence and can have a significant effect on the conclusions that can be drawn from the data. Types of missing data Missing data can occur because of nonresponse: no information is provided for several items or no information is provided for a whole unit.

Chapter 3. The IBM SPSS Statistics environment

1. In economics, _____ is a measure of relative satisfaction. Given this measure, one may speak meaningfully of increasing or decreasing _____, and thereby explain economic behavior in terms of attempts to increase one's _____. _____ is often modeled to be affected by consumption of various goods and services, possession of wealth and spending of leisure time.

   a. Allais paradox
   b. Utility
   c. Equity premium puzzle
   d. Exponential utility

2. In statistics, a _____ is a type of interval estimate of a population parameter and is used to indicate the reliability of an estimate. It is an observed interval (i.e. it is calculated from the observations), in principle different from sample to sample, that frequently includes the parameter of interest if the experiment is repeated. How frequently the observed interval contains the parameter is determined by the confidence level or confidence coefficient.

   a. Consensus forecast
   b. Constant elasticity of substitution
   c. Confidence interval
   d. Diversification

3. You may be looking for:

   · Chess _____ · Al-Fatiha, 'The _____', first chapter of the Qur'an. · _____ bid, a term from contract bridge. · Grand _____ of a business or other institution. · Vernissage, the _____ of an art exhibition. · _____, a morphological filtering operation used in image processing. · The _____ credits or title sequence of a TV show or film. · _____ statement, a beginning statement in a court case. '

   a. Apeirogon
   b. Equilateral pentagon
   c. Opening
   d. Isothetic polygon

4. _____s are used to describe the main features of a collection of data in quantitative terms. _____s are distinguished from inferential statistics (or inductive statistics), in that _____s aim to quantitatively summarize a data set, rather than being used to support inferential statements about the population that the data are thought to represent. Even when a data analysis draws its main conclusions using inductive statistical analysis, _____s are generally presented along with more formal analyses.

   a. standard error
   b. Descriptive statistic
   c. Margin of error
   d. statistical error

5. In mathematics, a (real) _____ is a set of real numbers with the property that any number that lies between two numbers in the set is also included in the set. For example, the set of all numbers x satisfying $0 \leq x \leq 1$ is an _____ which contains 0 and 1, as well as all numbers between them. Other examples of _____s are the set of all real numbers $\mathbb{R}$, the set of all negative real numbers, and the empty set.

a. Open book decomposition
b. Unit interval
c. Delta method
d. Interval

1. b
2. c
3. c
4. b
5. d

You can take the complete Chapter Practice Test

for Chapter 3. The IBM SPSS Statistics environment
on all key terms, persons, places, and concepts.

Online 99 Cents

http://www.epub27.31.21776.3.cram101.com/

Use www.Cram101.com for all your study needs

including Cram101's online interactive problem solving labs in

chemistry, statistics, mathematics, and more.

Chapter 4. Exploring data with graphs

CHAPTER OUTLINE: KEY TERMS, PEOPLE, PLACES, CONCEPTS

Wright

Chartjunk

Histogram

SPSS

Frequency distribution

Autocorrelation

Boxplot

Bar chart

Error bar

Sphericity

Line chart

Dot plot

Matrix

Chapter 4. Exploring data with graphs

Wright	In software architecture, Wright is an architecture description language developed at Carnegie Mellon University. Wright formalizes a software architecture in terms of concepts such as components, connectors, roles, and ports. The dynamic behavior of different ports of an individual component is described using the Communicating Sequential Processes (CSP) process algebra.
Chartjunk	Chartjunk refers to all visual elements in charts and graphs that are not necessary to comprehend the information represented on the graph, unnecessary text or inappropriately complex fontfaces, ornamented chart axes and display frames, pictures or icons within data graphs, ornamental shading and unnecessary dimensions.
Histogram	In statistics, a histogram is a graphical representation showing a visual impression of the distribution of data. It is an estimate of the probability distribution of a continuous variable and was first introduced by Karl Pearson. A histogram consists of tabular frequencies, shown as adjacent rectangles, erected over discrete intervals (bins), with an area equal to the frequency of the observations in the interval.
SPSS	SPSS Statistics is a software package used for statistical analysis. It is now officially named 'IBM SPSS Statistics'. Companion products in the same family are used for survey authoring and deployment (IBM SPSS Data Collection), data mining (IBM SPSS Modeler), text analytics, and collaboration and deployment (batch and automated scoring services).
Frequency distribution	In statistics, a frequency distribution is an arrangement of the values that one or more variables take in a sample. Each entry in the table contains the frequency or count of the occurrences of values within a particular group or interval, and in this way, the table summarizes the distribution of values in the sample. Univariate frequency tables

A different tabulation scheme aggregates values into bins such that each bin encompasses a range of values. |
| Autocorrelation | Autocorrelation is the cross-correlation of a signal with itself. Informally, it is the similarity between observations as a function of the time separation between them. It is a mathematical tool for finding repeating patterns, such as the presence of a periodic signal which has been buried under noise, or identifying the missing fundamental frequency in a signal implied by its harmonic frequencies. |
| Boxplot | In descriptive statistics, a box plot is a convenient way of graphically depicting groups of numerical data through their five-number summaries: the smallest observation (sample minimum), lower quartile (Q1), median (Q2), upper quartile (Q3), and largest observation (sample maximum). A boxplot may also indicate which observations, if any, might be considered outliers. |

Chapter 4. Exploring data with graphs

Bar chart	A bar chart is a chart with rectangular bars with lengths proportional to the values that they represent. The bars can be plotted vertically or horizontally. A vertical bar chart is sometimes called a column bar chart.
Error bar	Error bars are a graphical representation of the variability of data and are used on graphs to indicate the error, or uncertainty in a reported measurement. They give a general idea of how accurate a measurement is, or conversely, how far from the reported value the true (error free) value might be. Error bars often represent one standard deviation of uncertainty, one standard error, or a certain confidence interval (e.g., a 95% interval).
Sphericity	Sphericity is a measure of how spherical (round) an object is. As such, it is a specific example of a compactness measure of a shape. Defined by Wadell in 1935, the sphericity, Ψ, of a particle is: the ratio of the surface area of a sphere (with the same volume as the given particle) to the surface area of the particle: $$\Psi = \frac{\pi^{\frac{1}{3}}(6V_p)^{\frac{2}{3}}}{A_p}$$ where V_p is volume of the particle and A_p is the surface area of the particle.
Line chart	A line chart is a type of chart which displays information as a series of data points connected by straight line segments. It is a basic type of chart common in many fields. It is an extension of a scatter graph, and is created by connecting a series of points that represent individual measurements with line segments.
Dot plot	A dot chart or dot plot is a statistical chart consisting of data points plotted on a simple scale, typically using filled in circles. There are two common, yet very different, versions of the dot chart. The first is described by Wilkinson as a graph that has been used in hand-drawn (pre-computer era) graphs to depict distributions.
Matrix	In mathematics, a matrix is a rectangular array of numbers, symbols, or expressions, arranged in rows and columns. The individual items in a matrix are called its elements or entries. An example of a matrix with 2 rows and 3 columns is $\begin{bmatrix} 1 & 9 & -13 \\ 20 & 5 & -6 \end{bmatrix}$. Matrices of the same size can be added or subtracted element by element.

Chapter 4. Exploring data with graphs

1. _____ Statistics is a software package used for statistical analysis. It is now officially named 'IBM _____ Statistics'. Companion products in the same family are used for survey authoring and deployment (IBM _____ Data Collection), data mining (IBM _____ Modeler), text analytics, and collaboration and deployment (batch and automated scoring services).

   a. StatCVS
   b. Statgraphics
   c. SPSS
   d. StatPlus

2. In software architecture, _____ is an architecture description language developed at Carnegie Mellon University. _____ formalizes a software architecture in terms of concepts such as components, connectors, roles, and ports. The dynamic behavior of different ports of an individual component is described using the Communicating Sequential Processes (CSP) process algebra.

   a. Wright
   b. 4-dimensional Euclidean space
   c. Bacterial growth
   d. Balanced design

3. In statistics, a _____ is an arrangement of the values that one or more variables take in a sample. Each entry in the table contains the frequency or count of the occurrences of values within a particular group or interval, and in this way, the table summarizes the distribution of values in the sample. Univariate frequency tables

   A different tabulation scheme aggregates values into bins such that each bin encompasses a range of values.

   a. Lorenz asymmetry coefficient
   b. Frequency distribution
   c. Mean reciprocal rank
   d. Multiple of the median

4. _____ refers to all visual elements in charts and graphs that are not necessary to comprehend the information represented on the graph, unnecessary text or inappropriately complex fontfaces, ornamented chart axes and display frames, pictures or icons within data graphs, ornamental shading and unnecessary dimensions.

   a. Baby on board
   b. Bullet graph
   c. Bumper sticker
   d. Chartjunk

5. . A _____ is a chart with rectangular bars with lengths proportional to the values that they represent. The bars can be plotted vertically or horizontally. A vertical _____ is sometimes called a column _____.

   a. Barber-Johnson diagram

b. Bland-Altman plot

c. Box plot

d. Bar chart

1. c
2. a
3. b
4. d
5. d

You can take the complete Chapter Practice Test

for Chapter 4. Exploring data with graphs
on all key terms, persons, places, and concepts.

Online 99 Cents

http://www.epub27.31.21776.4.cram101.com/

Use www.Cram101.com for all your study needs

including Cram101's online interactive problem solving labs in

chemistry, statistics, mathematics, and more.

Chapter 5. The beast of bias

CHAPTER OUTLINE: KEY TERMS, PEOPLE, PLACES, CONCEPTS

	Bias
	Linear model
	Parameter
	Additivity
	Factorial ANOVA
	Homogeneity
	Homoscedastic
	Outlier
	Variance
	Confidence interval
	Interval
	Least squares
	Hypothetico-deductive model
	Normal distribution
	Null hypothesis
	ANOVA
	Central limit theorem
	Distribution
	Sphericity

P-P plot

Continuity correction

Kolmogorov-Smirnov test

Shapiro-Wilk test

Q-Q plot

Kurtosis

Skewness

Probability distribution

Residual

Levene's test

M-estimator

Truncated mean

Bonferroni correction

Wright

F-test

Square root

Transformation

Chapter 5. The beast of bias

Bias	A statistic is biased if it is calculated in such a way that is systematically different from the population parameter of interest. The following lists some types of, or aspects of, bias which should not be considered mutually exclusive:•Selection bias, where individuals or groups are more likely to take part in a research project than others, resulting in biased samples. This can also be termed Berksonian bias.
Linear model	In statistics, the term linear model is used in different ways according to the context. The most common occurrence is in connection with regression models and the term is often taken as synonymous with linear regression model. However, the term is also used in time series analysis with a different meaning.
Parameter	Parameter can be interpreted in mathematics, logic, linguistics, environmental science and other disciplines. In its common meaning, the term is used to identify a characteristic, a feature, a measurable factor that can help in defining a particular system. It is an important element to take into consideration for the evaluation or for the comprehension of an event, a project or any situation.
Additivity	In mathematics, additivity and sigma additivity of a function defined on subsets of a given set are abstractions of the intuitive properties of size (length, area, volume) of a set. Let μ be a function defined on an algebra of sets $\boxtimes$ $-\infty, +\infty]$. The function μ is called additive if, whenever A and B are disjoint sets in $\boxtimes$ $\boxtimes$ (A consequence of this is that an additive function cannot take both $-\infty$ and $+\infty$ as values, for the expression $\infty - \infty$ is undefined).
Factorial ANOVA	Factorial ANOVA is used when the experimenter wants to study the effects of two or more treatment variables. The most commonly used type of Factorial ANOVA is the 2^2 (read 'two by two') design, where there are two independent variables and each variable has two levels or distinct values. However, such use of ANOVA for analysis of 2^k factorial designs and fractional factorial designs is 'confusing and makes little sense'; instead it is suggested to refer the value of the effect divided by its standard error to a t-table. Factorial ANOVA can also be multi-level such as 3^3, etc. or higher order such as 2×2×2, etc.. Since the introduction of data analytic software, the utilization of higher order designs and analyses has become quite common.
Homogeneity	In statistics, homogeneity and its opposite, heterogeneity, arise in describing the properties of a dataset, or several datasets. They relate to the validity of the often convenient assumption that the statistical properties of any one part of an overall dataset are the same as any other part.

Chapter 5. The beast of bias

Homoscedastic	In statistics, a sequence or a vector of random variables is homoscedastic if all random variables in the sequence or vector have the same finite variance. This is also known as homogeneity of variance. The complementary notion is called heteroscedasticity.
Outlier	In statistics, an outlier is an observation that is numerically distant from the rest of the data. Grubbs defined an outlier as:' An outlying observation, or outlier, is one that appears to deviate markedly from other members of the sample in which it occurs. ' Outliers can occur by chance in any distribution, but they are often indicative either of measurement error or that the population has a heavy-tailed distribution.
Variance	In probability theory and statistics, the variance is a measure of how far a set of numbers is spread out. It is one of several descriptors of a probability distribution, describing how far the numbers lie from the mean (expected value). In particular, the variance is one of the moments of a distribution.
Confidence interval	In statistics, a confidence interval is a type of interval estimate of a population parameter and is used to indicate the reliability of an estimate. It is an observed interval (i.e. it is calculated from the observations), in principle different from sample to sample, that frequently includes the parameter of interest if the experiment is repeated. How frequently the observed interval contains the parameter is determined by the confidence level or confidence coefficient.
Interval	In mathematics, a (real) interval is a set of real numbers with the property that any number that lies between two numbers in the set is also included in the set. For example, the set of all numbers x satisfying $0 \leq x \leq 1$ is an interval which contains 0 and 1, as well as all numbers between them. Other examples of intervals are the set of all real numbers $\mathbb{R}$, the set of all negative real numbers, and the empty set.
Least squares	In mathematics, the idea of least squares can be applied to approximating a given function by a weighted sum of other functions. The best approximation can be defined as that which minimises the difference between the original function and the approximation; for a least-squares approach the quality of the approximation is measured in terms of the squared differences the two. Functional analysis A generalization to approximation of a data set is the approximation of a function by a sum of other functions, usually an orthogonal set: $$f(x) \approx f_n(x) = a_1\phi_1(x) + a_2\phi_2(x) + \cdots + a_n\phi_n(x),$$ with the set of functions { $\phi_j(x)$ } an orthonormal set over the interval of interest,

Chapter 5. The beast of bias

CHAPTER HIGHLIGHTS & NOTES: KEY TERMS, PEOPLE, PLACES, CONCEPTS

Hypothetico-deductive model	The hypothetico-deductive model, first so-named by William Whewell, is a proposed description of scientific method. According to it, scientific inquiry proceeds by formulating a hypothesis in a form that could conceivably be falsified by a test on observable data. A test that could and does run contrary to predictions of the hypothesis is taken as a falsification of the hypothesis.
Normal distribution	In probability theory, the normal distribution is a continuous probability distribution that has a bell-shaped probability density function, known as the Gaussian function or informally the bell curve: $$f(x; \mu, \sigma^2) = \frac{1}{\sigma\sqrt{2\pi}} e^{-\frac{1}{2}\left(\frac{x-\mu}{\sigma}\right)^2}$$ The parameter μ is the mean or expectation (location of the peak) and σ^2 is the variance. σ is known as the standard deviation. The distribution with $\mu = 0$ and $\sigma^2 = 1$ is called the standard normal distribution or the unit normal distribution.
Null hypothesis	The practice of science involves formulating and testing hypotheses, statements that are capable of being proven false using a test of observed data. The null hypothesis typically corresponds to a general or default position. For example, the null hypothesis might be that there is no relationship between two measured phenomena or that a potential treatment has no effect.
ANOVA	In statistics, ANOVA is a collection of statistical models, and their associated procedures, in which the observed variance is partitioned into components due to different sources of variation. In its simplest form ANOVA provides a statistical test of whether or not the means of several groups are all equal, and therefore generalizes Student's two-sample t-test to more than two groups. ANOVAs are helpful because they possess a certain advantage over a two-sample t-test. Doing multiple two-sample t-tests would result in a largely increased chance of committing a type I error. For this reason, ANOVAs are useful in comparing three or more means. There are three conceptual classes of such models: · Fixed-effects models assume that the data came from normal populations which may differ only in their means. (Model 1) · Random effects models assume that the data describe a hierarchy of different populations whose differences are constrained by the hierarchy. (Model 2) · Mixed-effect models describe the situations where both fixed and random effects are present. (Model 3)
Central limit theorem	In probability theory, the central limit theorem states that, given certain conditions, the mean of a sufficiently large number of independent random variables, each with finite mean and variance, will be approximately normally distributed. The central limit theorem has a number of variants. In its common form, the random variables must be identically distributed.

Chapter 5. The beast of bias

Sphericity	Sphericity is a measure of how spherical (round) an object is. As such, it is a specific example of a compactness measure of a shape. Defined by Wadell in 1935, the sphericity, Ψ, of a particle is: the ratio of the surface area of a sphere (with the same volume as the given particle) to the surface area of the particle: $$\Psi = \frac{\pi^{\frac{1}{3}}(6V_p)^{\frac{2}{3}}}{A_p}$$ where V_p is volume of the particle and A_p is the surface area of the particle.
P-P plot	In statistics, a P-P plot is a probability plot for assessing how closely two data sets agree, which plots the two cumulative distribution functions against each other. The Q-Q plot is more widely used, but they are both referred to as 'the' probability plot, and are potentially confused. A P-P plot plots two cumulative distribution functions (cdfs) against each other: given two probability distributions, with cdfs 'F' and 'G', it plots $(F(z), G(z))$ as z ranges from $-\infty$ to ∞. As a cdf has range [0,1], the domain of this parametric graph is $(-\infty, \infty)$ and the range is the unit square $[0, 1] \times [0, 1]$. Thus for input z the output is the pair of numbers giving what percentage of f and what percentage of g fall at or below z.
Continuity correction	In probability theory, if a random variable X has a binomial distribution with parameters n and p, i.e., X is distributed as the number of 'successes' in n independent Bernoulli trials with probability p of success on each trial, then $P(X \le x) = P(X < x + 1)$ for any x ∈ {0, 1, 2, ... n}. If np and n(1 − p) are large (sometimes taken to mean ≥ 5), then the probability above is fairly well approximated by $P(Y \le x + 1/2)$ where Y is a normally distributed random variable with the same expected value and the same variance as X, i.e., E(Y) = np and var(Y) = np(1 − p). This addition of 1/2 to x is a continuity correction.
Kolmogorov-Smirnov test	In statistics, the Kolmogorov-Smirnov test is a nonparametric test for the equality of continuous, one-dimensional probability distributions that can be used to compare a sample with a reference probability distribution (one-sample K-S test), or to compare two samples (two-sample K-S test).

The Kolmogorov-Smirnov statistic quantifies a distance between the empirical distribution function of the sample and the cumulative distribution function of the reference distribution, or between the empirical distribution functions of two samples. The null distribution of this statistic is calculated under the null hypothesis that the samples are drawn from the same distribution (in the two-sample case) or that the sample is drawn from the reference distribution (in the one-sample case).

Shapiro-Wilk test

In statistics, the Shapiro-Wilk test tests the null hypothesis that a sample $x_1, .. x_n$ came from a normally distributed population. It was published in 1965 by Samuel Shapiro and Martin Wilk.

The test statistic is:

$$W = \frac{\left(\sum_{i=1}^{n} a_i x_{(i)}\right)^2}{\sum_{i=1}^{n}(x_i - \overline{x})^2}$$

where• $x_{(i)}$ (with parentheses enclosing the subscript index i) is the ith order statistic, i.e., the ith-smallest number in the sample;• $\overline{x} = (x_1 + \ldots + x_n)/n$ is the sample mean;•the constants a_i are given by

$$(a_1, \ldots, a_n) = \frac{m^\top V^{-1}}{(m^\top V^{-1} V^{-1} m)^{1/2}}$$

$m = (m_1, \ldots, m_n)^\top$ and $m_1, .. m_n$ are the expected values of the order statistics of independent and identically distributed random variables sampled from the standard normal distribution, and V is the covariance matrix of those order statistics.

The user may reject the null hypothesis if W is too small.

Q-Q plot

In statistics, a Q-Q plot is a probability plot, which is a graphical method for comparing two probability distributions by plotting their quantiles against each other. First, the set of intervals for the quantiles are chosen. A point (x,y) on the plot corresponds to one of the quantiles of the second distribution (y-coordinate) plotted against the same quantile of the first distribution (x-coordinate).

Kurtosis

In probability theory and statistics, kurtosis is any measure of the 'peakedness' of the probability distribution of a real-valued random variable. In a similar way to the concept of skewness, kurtosis is a descriptor of the shape of a probability distribution and, just as for skewness, there are different ways of quantifying it for a theoretical distribution and corresponding ways of estimating it from a sample from a population. There are various interpretations of kurtosis, and of how particular measures should be interpreted; these are primarily peakedness (width of peak), tail weight, and lack of shoulders (distribution primarily peak and tails, not in between).

Chapter 5. The beast of bias

Skewness	In probability theory and statistics, skewness is a measure of the asymmetry of the probability distribution of a real-valued random variable. The skewness value can be positive or negative, or even undefined. Qualitatively, a negative skew indicates that the tail on the left side of the probability density function is longer than the right side and the bulk of the values (possibly including the median) lie to the right of the mean. A positive skew indicates that the tail on the right side is longer than the left side and the bulk of the values lie to the left of the mean. A zero value indicates that the values are relatively evenly distributed on both sides of the mean, typically (but not necessarily) implying a symmetric distribution.
Probability distribution	In probability and statistics, a probability distribution assigns a probability to each of the possible outcomes of a random experiment. Examples are found in experiments whose sample space is non-numerical, where the distribution would be a categorical distribution; experiments whose sample space is encoded by discrete random variables, where the distribution is a probability mass function; and experiments with sample spaces encoded by continuous random variables, where the distribution is a probability density function. More complex experiments, such as those involving stochastic processes defined in continuous-time, may demand the use of more general probability measures.
Residual	Loosely speaking, a residual is the error in a result. To be precise, suppose we want to find x such that $f(x) = b.$ Given an approximation x_0 of x, the residual is $b - f(x_0)$ whereas the error is $x_0 - x.$ If we do not know x, we cannot compute the error but we can compute the residual. Residual of the approximation of a function Similar terminology is used dealing with differential, integral and functional equations.
Levene's test	In statistics, Levene's test is an inferential statistic used to assess the equality of variances in different samples. Some common statistical procedures assume that variances of the populations from which different samples are drawn are equal. Levene's test assesses this assumption.
M-estimator	In statistics, M-estimators are a broad class of estimators, which are obtained as the minima of sums of functions of the data. Least-squares estimators and many maximum-likelihood estimators are M-estimators. The definition of M-estimators was motivated by robust statistics, which contributed new types of M-estimators.
Truncated mean	A truncated mean is a statistical measure of central tendency, much like the mean and median.

Chapter 5. The beast of bias

CHAPTER HIGHLIGHTS & NOTES: KEY TERMS, PEOPLE, PLACES, CONCEPTS

	It involves the calculation of the mean after discarding given parts of a probability distribution or sample at the high and low end, and typically discarding an equal amount of both.
	For most statistical applications, 5 to 25 percent of the ends are discarded.
Bonferroni correction	In statistics, the Bonferroni correction is a method used to counteract the problem of multiple comparisons. It is considered the simplest and most conservative method to control the familywise error rate. Informal introduction
	Statistical inference logic is based on rejecting the null hypotheses if the likelihood under the null hypotheses of the observed data is low.
Wright	In software architecture, Wright is an architecture description language developed at Carnegie Mellon University. Wright formalizes a software architecture in terms of concepts such as components, connectors, roles, and ports. The dynamic behavior of different ports of an individual component is described using the Communicating Sequential Processes (CSP) process algebra.
F-test	An F-test is any statistical test in which the test statistic has an F-distribution under the null hypothesis. It is most often used when comparing statistical models that have been fit to a data set, in order to identify the model that best fits the population from which the data were sampled. Exact F-tests mainly arise when the models have been fit to the data using least squares.
Square root	In mathematics, a square root of a number x is a number r such that r^2 = x, or, in other words, a number r whose square (the result of multiplying the number by itself, or r × r) is x.
	Every non-negative real number x has a unique non-negative square root, called the principal square root, denoted by a radical sign as $\sqrt{x}$. For positive x, the principal square root can also be written in exponent notation, as $x^{1/2}$.
Transformation	In combinatorial mathematics, the notion of transformation is used with several slightly different meanings. Informally, a transformation of a set of N values is an arrangement of those values into a particular order, where values may be repeated, but the ordered list is N elements in length. Thus, there are 27 transformations of the set {1,2,3}, namely [1,1,1], [1,1,2], [1,1,3], [1,2,1], [1,2,2], [1,2,3], [1,3,1],[1,3,2], [1,3,3], [2,1,1], [2,1,2],[2,1,3],[2,2,1], [2,2,2], [2,2,3], [2,3,1], [2,3,2], [2,3,3], [3,1,1], [3,1,2], [3,1,3], [3,2,1], [3,2,2], [3,2,3], [3,3,1], [3,3,2], and [3,3,3].

Chapter 5. The beast of bias

1. In statistics, the term _____ is used in different ways according to the context. The most common occurrence is in connection with regression models and the term is often taken as synonymous with linear regression model. However, the term is also used in time series analysis with a different meaning.

   a. Linear model
   b. Multicollinearity
   c. Multinomial probit
   d. Multiple correlation

2. A statistic is biased if it is calculated in such a way that is systematically different from the population parameter of interest. The following lists some types of, or aspects of, _____ which should not be considered mutually exclusive:•Selection _____, where individuals or groups are more likely to take part in a research project than others, resulting in biased samples. This can also be termed Berksonian _____.

   a. Bias
   b. Completeness
   c. Consistency
   d. Factorial experiment

3. In probability theory, the _____ is a continuous probability distribution that has a bell-shaped probability density

$$f(x;\mu,\sigma^2) = \frac{1}{\sigma\sqrt{2\pi}}e^{-\frac{1}{2}\left(\frac{x-\mu}{\sigma}\right)^2}$$

   function, known as the Gaussian function or informally the bell curve:

   The parameter μ is the mean or expectation (location of the peak) and $\sigma^{?2}$ is the variance. σ is known as the standard deviation. The distribution with $\mu = 0$ and $\sigma^{?2} = 1$ is called the standard _____ or the unit _____.

   a. Poisson distribution
   b. Normal distribution
   c. Models of scientific inquiry
   d. Multiple discovery

4. . In probability and statistics, a _____ assigns a probability to each of the possible outcomes of a random experiment. Examples are found in experiments whose sample space is non-numerical, where the distribution would be a categorical distribution; experiments whose sample space is encoded by discrete random variables, where the distribution is a probability mass function; and experiments with sample spaces encoded by continuous random variables, where the distribution is a probability density function. More complex experiments, such as those involving stochastic processes defined in continuous-time, may demand the use of more general probability measures.

   a. Random variable
   b. Probability distribution
   c. 4-dimensional Euclidean space

5. _____ can be interpreted in mathematics, logic, linguistics, environmental science and other disciplines.

In its common meaning, the term is used to identify a characteristic, a feature, a measurable factor that can help in defining a particular system. It is an important element to take into consideration for the evaluation or for the comprehension of an event, a project or any situation.

a. Parts-per notation
b. Pathological
c. Pivotal quantity
d. Parameter

1. a

2. a

3. b

4. b

5. d

You can take the complete Chapter Practice Test

for Chapter 5. The beast of bias
on all key terms, persons, places, and concepts.

Online 99 Cents

http://www.epub27.31.21776.5.cram101.com/

Use www.Cram101.com for all your study needs

including Cram101's online interactive problem solving labs in

chemistry, statistics, mathematics, and more.

CHAPTER OUTLINE: KEY TERMS, PEOPLE, PLACES, CONCEPTS

ANOVA

Factorial ANOVA

Statistical power

SPSS

Mann-Whitney U

Test statistic

Tied rank

Monte Carlo method

Effect size

Wilcoxon signed-rank test

McNemar's test

Sign test

Q-Q plot

Median test

Levene's test

Kendall's W

Chapter 6. Non-parametric models

ANOVA	In statistics, ANOVA is a collection of statistical models, and their associated procedures, in which the observed variance is partitioned into components due to different sources of variation. In its simplest form ANOVA provides a statistical test of whether or not the means of several groups are all equal, and therefore generalizes Student's two-sample t-test to more than two groups. ANOVAs are helpful because they possess a certain advantage over a two-sample t-test. Doing multiple two-sample t-tests would result in a largely increased chance of committing a type I error. For this reason, ANOVAs are useful in comparing three or more means.
	There are three conceptual classes of such models:
	· Fixed-effects models assume that the data came from normal populations which may differ only in their means. (Model 1) · Random effects models assume that the data describe a hierarchy of different populations whose differences are constrained by the hierarchy. (Model 2) · Mixed-effect models describe the situations where both fixed and random effects are present. (Model 3)
Factorial ANOVA	Factorial ANOVA is used when the experimenter wants to study the effects of two or more treatment variables. The most commonly used type of Factorial ANOVA is the 2^2 (read 'two by two') design, where there are two independent variables and each variable has two levels or distinct values. However, such use of ANOVA for analysis of 2^k factorial designs and fractional factorial designs is 'confusing and makes little sense'; instead it is suggested to refer the value of the effect divided by its standard error to a t-table. Factorial ANOVA can also be multi-level such as 3^3, etc. or higher order such as 2×2×2, etc.. Since the introduction of data analytic software, the utilization of higher order designs and analyses has become quite common.
Statistical power	The power of a statistical test is the probability that the test will reject the null hypothesis when the null hypothesis is actually false (i.e. the probability of not committing a Type II error, or making a false negative decision). The power is in general a function of the possible distributions, often determined by a parameter, under the alternative hypothesis. As the power increases, the chances of a Type II error occurring decrease. The probability of a Type II error occurring is referred to as the false negative rate (β). Therefore power is equal to $1 - \beta$, which is also known as the sensitivity.
	Power analysis can be used to calculate the minimum sample size required so that one can be reasonably likely to detect an effect of a given size. Power analysis can also be used to calculate the minimum effect size that is likely to be detected in a study using a given sample size. In addition, the concept of power is used to make comparisons between different statistical testing procedures: for example, between a parametric and a nonparametric test of the same hypothesis. Background
	Statistical tests use data from samples to assess, or make inferences about, a population.

In the concrete setting of a two-sample comparison, the goal is to assess whether the mean values of some attribute obtained for individuals in two sub-populations differ. For example, to test the null hypothesis that the mean scores of men and women on a test do not differ, samples of men and women are drawn, the test is administered to them, and the mean score of one group is compared to that of the other group using a statistical test such as the two-sample z-test. The power of the test is the probability that the test will find a statistically significant difference between men and women, as a function of the size of the true difference between those two populations. Note that power is the probability of finding a difference that does exist, as opposed to the likelihood of declaring a difference that does not exist (which is known as a Type I error, or 'false positive'). Factors influencing power

Statistical power may depend on a number of factors.

SPSS

SPSS Statistics is a software package used for statistical analysis. It is now officially named 'IBM SPSS Statistics'. Companion products in the same family are used for survey authoring and deployment (IBM SPSS Data Collection), data mining (IBM SPSS Modeler), text analytics, and collaboration and deployment (batch and automated scoring services).

Mann-Whitney U

In statistics, the Mann-Whitney U test is a non-parametric statistical hypothesis test for assessing whether one of two samples of independent observations tends to have larger values than the other. It is one of the most well-known non-parametric significance tests. It was proposed initially by the German Gustav Deuchler in 1914 (with a missing term in the variance) and later independently by Frank Wilcoxon in 1945, for equal sample sizes, and extended to arbitrary sample sizes and in other ways by Henry Mann and his student Donald Ransom Whitney in 1947.

Test statistic

In statistical hypothesis testing, a hypothesis test is typically specified in terms of a test statistic, which is a function of the sample; it is considered as a numerical summary of a set of data that reduces the data to one or a small number of values that can be used to perform a hypothesis test. Given a null hypothesis and a test statistic T, we can specify a 'null value' T_0 such that values of T close to T_0 present the strongest evidence in favor of the null hypothesis, whereas values of T far from T_0 present the strongest evidence against the null hypothesis. An important property of a test statistic is that we must be able to determine its sampling distribution under the null hypothesis, which allows us to calculate p-values.

Tied rank

Tied rank refers if two distinct obsevations have the same value, thus being given the same rank, they are said to be tied. This represents difficulties in the Wilcoxon two-sample test, the sign test, and the Fisher-Irwin test.

Monte Carlo method

Monte Carlo methods are a class of computational algorithms that rely on repeated random sampling to compute their results.

Chapter 6. Non-parametric models

Monte Carlo methods are often used in computer simulations of physical and mathematical systems. These methods are most suited to calculation by a computer and tend to be used when it is infeasible to compute an exact result with a deterministic algorithm.

Effect size	In statistics, an effect size is a measure of the strength of a phenomenon (for example, the relationship between two variables in a statistical population) or a sample-based estimate of that quantity. An effect size calculated from data is a descriptive statistic that conveys the estimated magnitude of a relationship without making any statement about whether the apparent relationship in the data reflects a true relationship in the population. In that way, effect sizes complement inferential statistics such as p-values.
Wilcoxon signed-rank test	The Wilcoxon signed-rank test is a non-parametric statistical hypothesis test used when comparing two related samples, matched samples, or repeated measurements on a single sample to assess whether their population mean ranks differ (i.e. it is a paired difference test). It can be used as an alternative to the paired Student's t-test, t-test for matched pairs, or the t-test for dependent samples when the population cannot be assumed to be normally distributed.
	The test is named for Frank Wilcoxon (1892-1965) who, in a single paper, proposed both it and the rank-sum test for two independent samples (Wilcoxon, 1945).
McNemar's test	In statistics, McNemar's test is a non-parametric method used on nominal data. It is applied to 2 × 2 contingency tables with a dichotomous trait, with matched pairs of subjects, to determine whether the row and column marginal frequencies are equal ('marginal homogeneity'). It is named after Quinn McNemar, who introduced it in 1947. An application of the test in genetics is the transmission disequilibrium test for detecting genetic linkage.
Sign test	In statistics, the sign test can be used to test the hypothesis that there is 'no difference in medians' between the continuous distributions of two random variables X and Y, in the situation when we can draw paired samples from X and Y. It is a non-parametric test which makes very few assumptions about the nature of the distributions under test - this means that it has very general applicability but may lack the statistical power of other tests such as the paired-samples t-test or the Wilcoxon signed-rank test. Method
	Let $p = \Pr(X > Y)$, and then test the null hypothesis H_0: $p = 0.50$. In other words, the null hypothesis states that given a random pair of measurements (x_i, y_i), then x_i and y_i are equally likely to be larger than the other.
	To test the null hypothesis, independent pairs of sample data are collected from the populations $\{(x_1, y_1), (x_2, y_2), .$

Chapter 6. Non-parametric models

Q-Q plot	In statistics, a Q-Q plot is a probability plot, which is a graphical method for comparing two probability distributions by plotting their quantiles against each other. First, the set of intervals for the quantiles are chosen. A point (x,y) on the plot corresponds to one of the quantiles of the second distribution (y-coordinate) plotted against the same quantile of the first distribution (x-coordinate).
Median test	In statistics, Mood's median test is a special case of Pearson's chi-squared test. It is a nonparametric test that tests the null hypothesis that the medians of the populations from which two samples are drawn are identical. The data in each sample are assigned to two groups, one consisting of data whose values are higher than the median value in the two groups combined, and the other consisting of data whose values are at the median or below.
Levene's test	In statistics, Levene's test is an inferential statistic used to assess the equality of variances in different samples. Some common statistical procedures assume that variances of the populations from which different samples are drawn are equal. Levene's test assesses this assumption.
Kendall's W	Kendall's W is a non-parametric statistic. It is a normalization of the statistic of the Friedman test, and can be used for assessing agreement among raters. Kendall's W ranges from 0 (no agreement) to 1 (complete agreement).

1. _____s are a class of computational algorithms that rely on repeated random sampling to compute their results. _____s are often used in computer simulations of physical and mathematical systems. These methods are most suited to calculation by a computer and tend to be used when it is infeasible to compute an exact result with a deterministic algorithm.

    a. Monte Carlo method
    b. Snowball sampling
    c. Square root biased sampling
    d. Survey sampling

2. . In statistics, the _____ test is a non-parametric statistical hypothesis test for assessing whether one of two samples of independent observations tends to have larger values than the other. It is one of the most well-known non-parametric significance tests. It was proposed initially by the German Gustav Deuchler in 1914 (with a missing term in the variance) and later independently by Frank Wilcoxon in 1945, for equal sample sizes, and extended to arbitrary sample sizes and in other ways by Henry Mann and his student Donald Ransom Whitney in 1947.

    a. Binomial test

    b. Mann-Whitney U

    c. Statistical Solutions

    d. StatPlus

3. The power of a statistical test is the probability that the test will reject the null hypothesis when the null hypothesis is actually false (i.e. the probability of not committing a Type II error, or making a false negative decision). The power is in general a function of the possible distributions, often determined by a parameter, under the alternative hypothesis. As the power increases, the chances of a Type II error occurring decrease. The probability of a Type II error occurring is referred to as the false negative rate (β). Therefore power is equal to $1 - \beta$, which is also known as the sensitivity.

Power analysis can be used to calculate the minimum sample size required so that one can be reasonably likely to detect an effect of a given size. Power analysis can also be used to calculate the minimum effect size that is likely to be detected in a study using a given sample size. In addition, the concept of power is used to make comparisons between different statistical testing procedures: for example, between a parametric and a nonparametric test of the same hypothesis. Background

Statistical tests use data from samples to assess, or make inferences about, a population. In the concrete setting of a two-sample comparison, the goal is to assess whether the mean values of some attribute obtained for individuals in two sub-populations differ. For example, to test the null hypothesis that the mean scores of men and women on a test do not differ, samples of men and women are drawn, the test is administered to them, and the mean score of one group is compared to that of the other group using a statistical test such as the two-sample z-test. The power of the test is the probability that the test will find a statistically significant difference between men and women, as a function of the size of the true difference between those two populations. Note that power is the probability of finding a difference that does exist, as opposed to the likelihood of declaring a difference that does not exist (which is known as a Type I error, or 'false positive'). Factors influencing power

_____ may depend on a number of factors.

    a. Statistical significance

    b. Test statistic

    c. Statistical power

    d. Closed testing procedure

4. . In statistics, _____ is a collection of statistical models, and their associated procedures, in which the observed variance is partitioned into components due to different sources of variation. In its simplest form _____ provides a statistical test of whether or not the means of several groups are all equal, and therefore generalizes Student's two-sample t-test to more than two groups. _____s are helpful because they possess a certain advantage over a two-sample t-test. Doing multiple two-sample t-tests would result in a largely increased chance of committing a type I error. For this reason, _____s are useful in comparing three or more means.

There are three conceptual classes of such models:

· Fixed-effects models assume that the data came from normal populations which may differ only in their means. (Model 1) · Random effects models assume that the data describe a hierarchy of different populations whose differences are constrained by the hierarchy. (Model 2) · Mixed-effect models describe the situations where both fixed and random effects are present. (Model 3)

a. Analysis of variance
b. ANOVA
c. axial
d. initial condition

5. In statistics, the _____ can be used to test the hypothesis that there is 'no difference in medians' between the continuous distributions of two random variables X and Y, in the situation when we can draw paired samples from X and Y. It is a non-parametric test which makes very few assumptions about the nature of the distributions under test - this means that it has very general applicability but may lack the statistical power of other tests such as the paired-samples t-test or the Wilcoxon signed-rank test. Method

Let $p = Pr(X > Y)$, and then test the null hypothesis H_0: $p = 0.50$. In other words, the null hypothesis states that given a random pair of measurements (x_i, y_i), then x_i and y_i are equally likely to be larger than the other.

To test the null hypothesis, independent pairs of sample data are collected from the populations $\{(x_1, y_1), (x_2, y_2), \cdot$

a. Spearman's rank correlation coefficient
b. Sign test
c. Van der Waerden test
d. Wald test

1. a
2. b
3. c
4. b
5. b

You can take the complete Chapter Practice Test

for Chapter 6. Non-parametric models
on all key terms, persons, places, and concepts.

Online 99 Cents

http://www.epub27.31.21776.6.cram101.com/

Use www.Cram101.com for all your study needs

including Cram101's online interactive problem solving labs in

chemistry, statistics, mathematics, and more.

Chapter 7. Correlation

_____ | Correlation

_____ | General linear model

_____ | Linear model

_____ | Cronbach's alpha

_____ | Covariance

_____ | Standard deviation

_____ | Big Brother

_____ | Ronald Aylmer Fisher

_____ | Semipartial correlation

_____ | Confidence interval

_____ | Interval

_____ | SPSS

_____ | Causality

_____ | Spearman's rank correlation coefficient

_____ | Coefficient

_____ | Coefficient of determination

_____ | Partial correlation

_____ | Effect size

_____ | Trait

CHAPTER OUTLINE: KEY TERMS, PEOPLE, PLACES, CONCEPTS

Wright

CHAPTER HIGHLIGHTS & NOTES: KEY TERMS, PEOPLE, PLACES, CONCEPTS

Correlation	In statistics, correlation (often measured as a correlation coefficient, ρ) indicates the strength and direction of a relationship between two random variables. The commonest use refers to a linear relationship. In general statistical usage, correlation or co-relation refers to the departure of two random variables from independence.
General linear model	The general linear model is a statistical linear model. It may be written as $\mathbf{Y} = \mathbf{XB} + \mathbf{U},$ where Y is a matrix with series of multivariate measurements, X is a matrix that might be a design matrix, B is a matrix containing parameters that are usually to be estimated and U is a matrix containing errors or noise. The errors are usually assumed to follow a multivariate normal distribution.
Linear model	In statistics, the term linear model is used in different ways according to the context. The most common occurrence is in connection with regression models and the term is often taken as synonymous with linear regression model. However, the term is also used in time series analysis with a different meaning.
Cronbach's alpha	Cronbach's α (alpha) is a coefficient of reliability. It is commonly used as a measure of the internal consistency or reliability of a psychometric test score for a sample of examinees. It was first named alpha by Lee Cronbach in 1951, as he had intended to continue with further coefficients. The measure can be viewed as an extension of the Kuder-Richardson Formula 20 (KR-20), which is an equivalent measure for dichotomous items. Alpha is not robust against missing data. Several other Greek letters have been used by later researchers to designate other measures used in a similar context. Somewhat related is the average variance extracted (AVE). Cronbach's α is defined as $$\alpha = \frac{K}{K-1}\left(1 - \frac{\sum_{i=1}^{K}\sigma_{Y_i}^2}{\sigma_X^2}\right)$$

Chapter 7. Correlation

where K is the number of components (K-items or testlets), σ^2_X the variance of the observed total test scores, and $\sigma^2_{Y_i}$ the variance of component i for the current sample of persons.

Alternatively, the Cronbach's α can also be defined as
$$\alpha = \frac{K\bar{c}}{(\bar{v} + (K-1)\bar{c})}$$

where K is as above, $\bar{v}$ the average variance, and $\bar{c}$ the average of all covariances between the components across the current sample of persons.

The standardized Cronbach's alpha can be defined as
$$\alpha_{\text{standardized}} = \frac{K\bar{r}}{(1 + (K-1)\bar{r})}$$

where K is as above and $\bar{r}$ the mean of the K(K − 1) / 2 non-redundant correlation coefficients (i.e., the mean of an upper triangular, or lower triangular, correlation matrix).

Covariance	In probability theory and statistics, covariance is a measure of how much two random variables change together. If the greater values of one variable mainly correspond with the greater values of the other variable, and the same holds for the smaller values, i.e., the variables tend to show similar behavior, the covariance is positive. In the opposite case, when the greater values of one variable mainly correspond to the smaller values of the other, i.e., the variables tend to show opposite behavior, the covariance is negative.
Standard deviation	In statistics and probability theory, standard deviation shows how much variation or 'dispersion' exists from the average (mean, or expected value). A low standard deviation indicates that the data points tend to be very close to the mean; high standard deviation indicates that the data points are spread out over a large range of values. The standard deviation of a random variable, statistical population, data set, or probability distribution is the square root of its variance.
Big Brother	Big Brother (alias BB) is a tool for systems and network monitoring, generally used by system administrators. The advent of the dynamic web page allowed Big Brother to be one of the first monitoring systems to use the web as its user interface. Prior to this, monitoring tools were generally console based, or required graphic terminals such as X Window to operate.
Ronald Aylmer Fisher	Sir Ronald Aylmer Fisher FRS (17 February 1890 - 29 July 1962) was an English statistician, evolutionary biologist, eugenicist and geneticist.

Chapter 7. Correlation

Semipartial correlation	Semipartial correlation is the correlation the independent with the dependent, controlling only the independent variable for control variables. In multiple regression, the squared semipartial correlation is the proportion of the total variance in the dependent variable accounted for by adding the given independent variable to those already entered in the multiple regression formula.
Confidence interval	In statistics, a confidence interval is a type of interval estimate of a population parameter and is used to indicate the reliability of an estimate. It is an observed interval (i.e. it is calculated from the observations), in principle different from sample to sample, that frequently includes the parameter of interest if the experiment is repeated. How frequently the observed interval contains the parameter is determined by the confidence level or confidence coefficient.
Interval	In mathematics, a (real) interval is a set of real numbers with the property that any number that lies between two numbers in the set is also included in the set. For example, the set of all numbers x satisfying $0 \leq x \leq 1$ is an interval which contains 0 and 1, as well as all numbers between them. Other examples of intervals are the set of all real numbers $\mathbb{R}$, the set of all negative real numbers, and the empty set.
SPSS	SPSS Statistics is a software package used for statistical analysis. It is now officially named 'IBM SPSS Statistics'. Companion products in the same family are used for survey authoring and deployment (IBM SPSS Data Collection), data mining (IBM SPSS Modeler), text analytics, and collaboration and deployment (batch and automated scoring services).
Causality	Causality is the relationship between an event (the cause) and a second event (the effect), where the second event is understood as a consequence of the first.

In common usage, causality is also the relationship between a set of factors (causes) and a phenomenon (the effect). Anything that affects an effect is a factor of that effect. |
| Spearman's rank correlation coefficient | In statistics, Spearman's rank correlation coefficient is a non-parametric measure of statistical dependence between two variables. It assesses how well the relationship between two variables can be described using a monotonic function. If there are no repeated data values, a perfect Spearman correlation of +1 or −1 occurs when each of the variables is a perfect monotone function of the other. |
| Coefficient | In mathematics, a Coefficient is a multiplicative factor in some term of an expression (or of a series); it is usually a number, but in any case does not involve any variables of the expression. For instance in

$7x^2 - 3xy + 1.5 + y$ |

Chapter 7. Correlation

the first three terms respectively have Coefficients 7, −3, and 1.5 (in the third term there are no variables, so the Coefficient is the term itself; it is called the constant term or constant Coefficient of this expression). The final term does not have any explicitly written Coefficient, but is usually considered to have Coefficient 1, since multiplying by that factor would not change the term.

Coefficient of determination

In statistics, the coefficient of determination, denoted R^2, is used in the context of statistical models whose main purpose is the prediction of future outcomes on the basis of other related information. R^2 is most often seen as a number between 0 and 1.0, used to describe how well a regression line fits a set of data. An R^2 near 1.0 indicates that a regression line fits the data well, while an R^2 closer to 0 indicates a regression line does not fit the data very well.

Partial correlation

In probability theory and statistics, partial correlation measures the degree of association between two random variables, with the effect of a set of controlling random variables removed. Formal definition

Formally, the partial correlation between X and Y given a set of n controlling variables $Z = \{Z_1, Z_2, ..., Z_n\}$, written $\rho_{XY \cdot Z}$, is the correlation between the residuals R_X and R_Y resulting from the linear regression of X with Z and of Y with Z, respectively. In fact, the first-order partial correlation is nothing else than a difference between a correlation and the product of the removable correlations divided by the product of the coefficients of alienation of the removable correlations.

Effect size

In statistics, an effect size is a measure of the strength of a phenomenon (for example, the relationship between two variables in a statistical population) or a sample-based estimate of that quantity. An effect size calculated from data is a descriptive statistic that conveys the estimated magnitude of a relationship without making any statement about whether the apparent relationship in the data reflects a true relationship in the population. In that way, effect sizes complement inferential statistics such as p-values.

Trait

In computer programming, a trait is a collection of methods, used as a 'simple conceptual model for structuring object oriented programs'. Traits are similar to mixins, but whereas mixins can be composed only using the inheritance operation, traits offer a much wider selection of operations, including symmetric sum, method exclusion, and aliasing. A Trait differs from an abstract type in that it provides implementations of its methods, not just type signatures.

Wright

In software architecture, Wright is an architecture description language developed at Carnegie Mellon University. Wright formalizes a software architecture in terms of concepts such as components, connectors, roles, and ports. The dynamic behavior of different ports of an individual component is described using the Communicating Sequential Processes (CSP) process algebra.

1. The _____ is a statistical linear model. It may be written as $Y = XB + U$,

where Y is a matrix with series of multivariate measurements, X is a matrix that might be a design matrix, B is a matrix containing parameters that are usually to be estimated and U is a matrix containing errors or noise. The errors are usually assumed to follow a multivariate normal distribution.

a. Generalized linear array model
b. Generalized multidimensional scaling
c. Geodemographic segmentation
d. General linear model

2. In statistics, an _____ is a measure of the strength of a phenomenon (for example, the relationship between two variables in a statistical population) or a sample-based estimate of that quantity. An _____ calculated from data is a descriptive statistic that conveys the estimated magnitude of a relationship without making any statement about whether the apparent relationship in the data reflects a true relationship in the population. In that way, _____s complement inferential statistics such as p-values.

a. Electronic common technical document
b. Electronic data capture
c. Effect size
d. Ethics committee

3. _____ (alias BB) is a tool for systems and network monitoring, generally used by system administrators. The advent of the dynamic web page allowed _____ to be one of the first monitoring systems to use the web as its user interface. Prior to this, monitoring tools were generally console based, or required graphic terminals such as X Window to operate.

a. Cacti
b. CONFER
c. Distributed File System
d. Big Brother

4. . In probability theory and statistics, _____ measures the degree of association between two random variables, with the effect of a set of controlling random variables removed. Formal definition

Formally, the _____ between X and Y given a set of n controlling variables Z = {Z_1, Z_2, ..., Z_n}, written $\rho_{XY \cdot Z}$, is the correlation between the residuals R_X and R_Y resulting from the linear regression of X with Z and of Y with Z, respectively. In fact, the first-order _____ is nothing else than a difference between a correlation and the product of the removable correlations divided by the product of the coefficients of alienation of the removable correlations.

a. Partial correlation
b. Rank correlation
c. Rational quadratic covariance function

Chapter 7. Correlation

CHAPTER QUIZ: KEY TERMS, PEOPLE, PLACES, CONCEPTS

5. In statistics, _____ (often measured as a _____ coefficient, ρ) indicates the strength and direction of a relationship between two random variables. The commonest use refers to a linear relationship. In general statistical usage, _____ or co-relation refers to the departure of two random variables from independence.

    a. Covariance matrix
    b. Pearson product-moment correlation coefficient
    c. Correlation
    d. Sample covariance matrix

ANSWER KEY
Chapter 7. Correlation

1. d
2. c
3. d
4. a
5. c

You can take the complete Chapter Practice Test

for Chapter 7. Correlation
on all key terms, persons, places, and concepts.

Online 99 Cents

http://www.epub27.31.21776.7.cram101.com/

Use www.Cram101.com for all your study needs

including Cram101's online interactive problem solving labs in

chemistry, statistics, mathematics, and more.

Chapter 8. Regression

CHAPTER OUTLINE: KEY TERMS, PEOPLE, PLACES, CONCEPTS

	Linear model
	Gradient
	Linear regression
	Regression coefficient
	Predictor variable
	Residual sum of squares
	Residual
	Goodness of fit
	Least squares
	Ordinary least squares
	Total sum of squares
	T-statistic
	T-test
	Outlier
	Cook's distance
	Levene's test
	Mahalanobis distance
	Leverage
	DFFITS

	Mortality
	Autocorrelation
	Normally distributed
	Regression
	Cronbach's alpha
	Cross-validation
	Factorial ANOVA
	Multicollinearity
	Shrinkage
	Sample size
	Sampling
	SPSS
	Multiple regression
	Stepwise regression
	Variance inflation factor
	Robust regression
	English
	Categorical data
	Eigenvalue

| | Frequency distribution |
| | Chaos |

CHAPTER HIGHLIGHTS & NOTES: KEY TERMS, PEOPLE, PLACES, CONCEPTS

Linear model	In statistics, the term linear model is used in different ways according to the context. The most common occurrence is in connection with regression models and the term is often taken as synonymous with linear regression model. However, the term is also used in time series analysis with a different meaning.
Gradient	In vector calculus, the gradient of a scalar field is a vector field which points in the direction of the greatest rate of increase of the scalar field, and whose magnitude is the greatest rate of change. A generalization of the gradient for functions on a Euclidean space which have values in another Euclidean space is the Jacobian. A further generalization for a function from one Banach space to another is the Fréchet derivative.
Linear regression	In statistics, linear regression is an approach to modeling the relationship between a scalar dependent variable y and one or more explanatory variables denoted X. The case of one explanatory variable is called simple regression. More than one explanatory variable is multiple regression. (This in turn should be distinguished from multivariate linear regression, where multiple correlated dependent variables are predicted, rather than a single scalar variable).
Regression coefficient	The regression coefficient is the slope of the straight line that most closely relates two correlated variables.
Predictor variable	The predictor variable is manipulated by the experimenter. By attempting to isolate all other factors, one can determine the influence of the independent variable on the dependent variable.
Residual sum of squares	In statistics, the residual sum of squares is the sum of squares of residuals. It is also known as the sum of squared residuals (SSR) or the sum of squared errors of prediction (SSE). It is a measure of the discrepancy between the data and an estimation model.

Chapter 8. Regression

Residual	Loosely speaking, a residual is the error in a result. To be precise, suppose we want to find x such that $f(x) = b.$
	Given an approximation x_0 of x, the residual is $b - f(x_0)$
	whereas the error is $x_0 - x.$
	If we do not know x, we cannot compute the error but we can compute the residual. Residual of the approximation of a function
	Similar terminology is used dealing with differential, integral and functional equations.
Goodness of fit	The goodness of fit of a statistical model describes how well it fits a set of observations. Measures of goodness of fit typically summarize the discrepancy between observed values and the values expected under the model in question. Such measures can be used in statistical hypothesis testing, e.g. to test for normality of residuals, to test whether two samples are drawn from identical distributions , or whether outcome frequencies follow a specified distribution .
Least squares	In mathematics, the idea of least squares can be applied to approximating a given function by a weighted sum of other functions. The best approximation can be defined as that which minimises the difference between the original function and the approximation; for a least-squares approach the quality of the approximation is measured in terms of the squared differences the two. Functional analysis
	A generalization to approximation of a data set is the approximation of a function by a sum of other functions, usually an orthogonal set: $$f(x) \approx f_n(x) = a_1\phi_1(x) + a_2\phi_2(x) + \cdots + a_n\phi_n(x),$$
	with the set of functions { $\phi_j(x)$ } an orthonormal set over the interval of interest, say [a, b].
Ordinary least squares	In statistics, ordinary least squares or linear least squares is a method for estimating the unknown parameters in a linear regression model. This method minimizes the sum of squared vertical distances between the observed responses in the dataset and the responses predicted by the linear approximation. The resulting estimator can be expressed by a simple formula, especially in the case of a single regressor on the right-hand side.
Total sum of squares	In statistical data analysis the total sum of squares is a quantity that appears as part of a standard way of presenting results of such analyses. It is defined as being the sum, over all observations, of the squared differences of each observation from the overall mean.

In statistical linear models, (particularly in standard regression models), the TSS is the sum of the

squares of the difference of the dependent variable and its grand mean: $\sum_{i=1}^{n} (y_i - \bar{y})^2$.

Where: $\bar{y}$ is the mean.

T-statistic

In statistics, the t-statistic is a ratio of the departure of an estimated parameter from its notional value and its standard error. It is used in hypothesis testing, for example in the Student's t-test, in the augmented Dickey-Fuller test, and in bootstrapping.

Let $\hat{\beta}$ be an estimator of parameter β in some statistical model.

T-test

A t-test is any statistical hypothesis test in which the test statistic follows a Student's t distribution if the null hypothesis is true. It is most commonly applied when the test statistic would follow a normal distribution if the value of a scaling term in the test statistic were known. When the scaling term is unknown and is replaced by an estimate based on the data, the test statistic (under certain conditions) follows a Student's t distribution.

Outlier

In statistics, an outlier is an observation that is numerically distant from the rest of the data. Grubbs defined an outlier as:'

An outlying observation, or outlier, is one that appears to deviate markedly from other members of the sample in which it occurs. '

Outliers can occur by chance in any distribution, but they are often indicative either of measurement error or that the population has a heavy-tailed distribution.

Cook's distance

In statistics, Cook's distance is a commonly used estimate of the influence of a data point when doing least squares regression analysis. In a practical ordinary least squares analysis, Cook's distance can be used in several ways: to indicate data points that are particularly worth checking for validity; to indicate regions of the design space where it would be good to be able obtain more data points.

Cook's distance measures the effect of deleting a given observation.

Levene's test

In statistics, Levene's test is an inferential statistic used to assess the equality of variances in different samples. Some common statistical procedures assume that variances of the populations from which different samples are drawn are equal.

Chapter 8. Regression

Mahalanobis distance	In statistics, Mahalanobis distance is a distance measure introduced by P. C. Mahalanobis in 1936. It is based on correlations between variables by which different patterns can be identified and analyzed. It gauges similarity of an unknown sample set to a known one. It differs from Euclidean distance in that it takes into account the correlations of the data set and is scale-invariant.
Leverage	In statistics, leverage is a term used in connection with regression analysis and, in particular, in analyses aimed at identifying those observations that are far away from corresponding average predictor values. Leverage points do not necessarily have a large effect on the outcome of fitting regression models. Leverage points are those observations, if any, made at extreme or outlying values of the independent variables such that the lack of neighboring observations means that the fitted regression model will pass close to that particular observation.
DFFITS	DFFITS is a diagnostic meant to show how influential a point is in a statistical regression. It was proposed in 1980. It is defined as the change ('DFFIT'), in the predicted value for a point, obtained when that point is left out of the regression, 'Studentized' by dividing by the estimated standard deviation of the fit at that point: $$DFFITS = \frac{\hat{y}_i - \widehat{y_{i(i)}}}{s_{(i)}\sqrt{h_{ii}}}$$ where $\hat{y}_i$ and $\widehat{y_{i(i)}}$ are the prediction for point i with and without point i included in the regression, $s_{(i)}$ is the standard error estimated without the point in question, and h_{ii} is the leverage for the point. DFFITS is very similar to the externally Studentized residual, and is in fact equal to the latter times $\sqrt{h_{ii}/(1-h_{ii})}$.
Mortality	In computability theory, the mortality problem is a decision problem which can be stated as follows: In the statement above, the configuration is a pair , where q is one of the machine's states (not necessarily its initial state) and w is an infinite sequence of symbols representing the initial content of the tape. Note that while we usually assume that in the starting configuration all but finitely many cells on the tape are blanks, in the mortality problem the tape can have arbitrary content, including infinitely many non-blank symbols written on it.

	Philip K. Hooper proved in 1966 that the mortality problem is undecidable.
Autocorrelation	Autocorrelation is the cross-correlation of a signal with itself. Informally, it is the similarity between observations as a function of the time separation between them. It is a mathematical tool for finding repeating patterns, such as the presence of a periodic signal which has been buried under noise, or identifying the missing fundamental frequency in a signal implied by its harmonic frequencies.
Normally distributed	In probability theory, the normal distribution is a continuous probability distribution, defined by the $$f(x) = \frac{1}{\sigma\sqrt{2\pi}} e^{-\frac{1}{2}\left(\frac{x-\mu}{\sigma}\right)^2}$$ formula
	The parameter μ in this formula is the mean or expectation of the distribution (and also its median and mode). The parameter σ is its standard deviation; its variance is therefore $\sigma^{?2}$. A random variable with a Gaussian distribution is said to be normally distributed and is called a normal deviate.
Regression	Regression in medicine is a characteristic of diseases to show lighter symptoms without completely disappearing. At a later point, symptoms may return. These symptoms are then called recidive.
Cronbach's alpha	Cronbach's α (alpha) is a coefficient of reliability. It is commonly used as a measure of the internal consistency or reliability of a psychometric test score for a sample of examinees. It was first named alpha by Lee Cronbach in 1951, as he had intended to continue with further coefficients. The measure can be viewed as an extension of the Kuder-Richardson Formula 20 (KR-20), which is an equivalent measure for dichotomous items. Alpha is not robust against missing data. Several other Greek letters have been used by later researchers to designate other measures used in a similar context. Somewhat related is the average variance extracted (AVE). $$\alpha = \frac{K}{K-1}\left(1 - \frac{\sum_{i=1}^{K} \sigma_{Y_i}^2}{\sigma_X^2}\right)$$ Cronbach's α is defined as
	where K is the number of components (K-items or testlets), σ_X^2 the variance of the observed total test scores, and $\sigma_{Y_i}^2$ the variance of component i for the current sample of persons.
	Alternatively, the Cronbach's α can also be defined as

Chapter 8. Regression

$$\alpha = \frac{K\bar{c}}{(\bar{v} + (K-1)\bar{c})}$$

where K is as above, $\bar{v}$ the average variance, and $\bar{c}$ the average of all covariances between the components across the current sample of persons.

The standardized Cronbach's alpha can be defined as

$$\alpha_{\text{standardized}} = \frac{K\bar{r}}{(1 + (K-1)\bar{r})}$$

where K is as above and $\bar{r}$ the mean of the $K(K-1)/2$ non-redundant correlation coefficients (i.e., the mean of an upper triangular, or lower triangular, correlation matrix).

Cross-validation	Cross-validation, sometimes called rotation estimation, is a technique for assessing how the results of a statistical analysis will generalize to an independent data set. It is mainly used in settings where the goal is prediction, and one wants to estimate how accurately a predictive model will perform in practice. One round of cross-validation involves partitioning a sample of data into complementary subsets, performing the analysis on one subset (called the training set), and validating the analysis on the other subset (called the validation set or testing set).
Factorial ANOVA	Factorial ANOVA is used when the experimenter wants to study the effects of two or more treatment variables. The most commonly used type of Factorial ANOVA is the 2^2 (read 'two by two') design, where there are two independent variables and each variable has two levels or distinct values. However, such use of ANOVA for analysis of 2^k factorial designs and fractional factorial designs is 'confusing and makes little sense'; instead it is suggested to refer the value of the effect divided by its standard error to a t-table. Factorial ANOVA can also be multi-level such as 3^3, etc. or higher order such as 2×2×2, etc.. Since the introduction of data analytic software, the utilization of higher order designs and analyses has become quite common.
Multicollinearity	Multicollinearity is a statistical phenomenon in which two or more predictor variables in a multiple regression model are highly correlated. In this situation the coefficient estimates may change erratically in response to small changes in the model or the data. Multicollinearity does not reduce the predictive power or reliability of the model as a whole, at least within the sample data themselves; it only affects calculations regarding individual predictors.
Shrinkage	In statistics, shrinkage has two meanings:•In relation to the general observation that, in regression analysis, a fitted relationship appears to perform less well on a new data set than on the data set used for fitting. In particular the value of the coefficient of determination 'shrinks'.

Sample size	Sample size determination is the act of choosing the number of observations or replicates to include in a statistical sample. The sample size is an important feature of any empirical study in which the goal is to make inferences about a population from a sample. In practice, the sample size used in a study is determined based on the expense of data collection, and the need to have sufficient statistical power.
Sampling	In statistics and survey methodology, sampling is concerned with the selection of a subset of individuals from within a population to estimate characteristics of the whole population. Researchers rarely survey the entire population because the cost of a census is too high. The three main advantages of sampling are that the cost is lower, data collection is faster, and since the data set is smaller it is possible to ensure homogeneity and to improve the accuracy and quality of the data.
SPSS	SPSS Statistics is a software package used for statistical analysis. It is now officially named 'IBM SPSS Statistics'. Companion products in the same family are used for survey authoring and deployment (IBM SPSS Data Collection), data mining (IBM SPSS Modeler), text analytics, and collaboration and deployment (batch and automated scoring services).
Multiple regression	In statistics, linear regression is an approach to modeling the relationship between a scalar dependent variable y and one or more explanatory variables denoted X. The case of one explanatory variable is called simple regression. More than one explanatory variable is multiple regression. (This in turn should be distinguished from multivariate linear regression, where multiple correlated dependent variables are predicted, rather than a single scalar variable).
Stepwise regression	In statistics, stepwise regression includes regression models in which the choice of predictive variables is carried out by an automatic procedure. Usually, this takes the form of a sequence of F-tests, but other techniques are possible, such as t-tests, adjusted R-square, Akaike information criterion, Bayesian information criterion, Mallows' Cp, or false discovery rate. The main approaches are:•Forward selection, which involves starting with no variables in the model, trying out the variables one by one and including them if they are 'statistically significant'.•Backward elimination, which involves starting with all candidate variables and testing them one by one for statistical significance, deleting any that are not significant.•Methods that are a combination of the above, testing at each stage for variables to be included or excluded. A widely used algorithm was first proposed by Efroymson (1960).
Variance inflation factor	In statistics, the variance inflation factor quantifies the severity of multicollinearity in an ordinary least squares regression analysis.

	It provides an index that measures how much the variance (the square of the estimate's standard deviation) of an estimated regression coefficient is increased because of collinearity.
	Consider the following linear model with k independent variables:$Y = \beta_0 + \beta_1 X_1 + \beta_2 X_2 + ... + \beta_k X_k + \varepsilon$.
	The standard error of the estimate of β_j is the square root of the j+1, j+1 element of $s^2(X'X)^{-1}$, where s is the root mean squared error (RMSE) (note that $RMSE^2$ is an unbiased estimator of the true variance of the error term, σ^2); X is the regression design matrix - a matrix such that $X_{i,\,j+1}$ is the value of the jth independent variable for the ith case or observation, and such that $X_{i,\,1}$ equals 1 for all i.
Robust regression	In robust statistics, robust regression is a form of regression analysis designed to circumvent some limitations of traditional parametric and non-parametric methods. Regression analysis seeks to find the relationship between one or more independent variables and a dependent variable. Certain widely used methods of regression, such as ordinary least squares, have favourable properties if their underlying assumptions are true, but can give misleading results if those assumptions are not true; thus ordinary least squares is said to be not robust to violations of its assumptions.
English	English is a database retrieval and reporting language somewhat like SQL, but with no programming or update abilities. It was originally released by Microdata in 1973 and named so that the company's brochures could claim that developers could generate reports on their implementation of the Pick operating system using English.
Categorical data	In statistics, categorical data is that part of an observed dataset that consists of categorical variables, or for data that has been converted into that form, for example as grouped data. More specifically, categorical data may derive from either or both of observations made of qualitative data, where the observations are summarised as counts or cross tabulations, or of quantitative data, where observations might be directly observed counts of events happening or they might counts of values that occur within given intervals. Often, purely categorical data are summarised in the form of a contingency table.
Eigenvalue	In mathematics, Eigenvalues, eigenvectors and eigenspaces are properties of a matrix. They are computed by a method described below, give important information about the matrix, and can be used in matrix factorization. They have applications in areas of applied mathematics as diverse as finance and quantum mechanics.
Frequency distribution	In statistics, a frequency distribution is an arrangement of the values that one or more variables take in a sample.

	Each entry in the table contains the frequency or count of the occurrences of values within a particular group or interval, and in this way, the table summarizes the distribution of values in the sample. Univariate frequency tables
	A different tabulation scheme aggregates values into bins such that each bin encompasses a range of values.
Chaos	Chaos in Greek mythology and cosmology referred to a gap or abyss at the beginning of the world, or more generally the initial, formless state of the universe. (the antithetical, or possibly complementary, concept was cosmos).
	Later uses of the term by philosophers varied over time.

1. In statistical data analysis the _____ is a quantity that appears as part of a standard way of presenting results of such analyses. It is defined as being the sum, over all observations, of the squared differences of each observation from the overall mean.

   In statistical linear models, (particularly in standard regression models), the TSS is the sum of the squares of the difference of the dependent variable and its grand mean: $\sum_{i=1}^{n} (y_i - \bar{y})^2$.

   Where: $\bar{y}$ is the mean.

   a. Trend analysis
   b. Variable rules analysis
   c. Total sum of squares
   d. Proportional hazards models

2. . In robust statistics, _____ is a form of regression analysis designed to circumvent some limitations of traditional parametric and non-parametric methods. Regression analysis seeks to find the relationship between one or more independent variables and a dependent variable. Certain widely used methods of regression, such as ordinary least squares, have favourable properties if their underlying assumptions are true, but can give misleading results if those assumptions are not true; thus ordinary least squares is said to be not robust to violations of its assumptions.

   a. Savitzky-Golay smoothing filter

    b. Robust regression

    c. Segmented regression

    d. Separation

3. In statistics, _____ is an approach to modeling the relationship between a scalar dependent variable y and one or more explanatory variables denoted X. The case of one explanatory variable is called simple regression. More than one explanatory variable is multiple regression. (This in turn should be distinguished from multivariate _____, where multiple correlated dependent variables are predicted, rather than a single scalar variable).

    a. Linear regression

    b. Matched filter

    c. Maximum likelihood

    d. Maximum spacing estimation

4. _____ is a database retrieval and reporting language somewhat like SQL, but with no programming or update abilities. It was originally released by Microdata in 1973 and named so that the company's brochures could claim that developers could generate reports on their implementation of the Pick operating system using _____.

    a. Abu Mansur Abd al-Qahir ibn Tahir ibn Muhammad ibn Abdallah al-Tamimi al-Shaffi al-Baghdadi

    b. English

    c. Segmented regression

    d. Separation

5. In statistics, the term _____ is used in different ways according to the context. The most common occurrence is in connection with regression models and the term is often taken as synonymous with linear regression model. However, the term is also used in time series analysis with a different meaning.

    a. Linear model

    b. Multicollinearity

    c. Multinomial probit

    d. Multiple correlation

ANSWER KEY
Chapter 8. Regression

1. c
2. b
3. a
4. b
5. a

You can take the complete Chapter Practice Test

for Chapter 8. Regression
on all key terms, persons, places, and concepts.

Online 99 Cents

http://www.epub27.31.21776.8.cram101.com/

Use **www.Cram101.com** for all your study needs

including **Cram101's online interactive problem solving labs in**

chemistry, statistics, mathematics, and more.

Chapter 9. Comparing two means

CHAPTER OUTLINE: KEY TERMS, PEOPLE, PLACES, CONCEPTS

Mahalanobis distance

Coefficient

Independent variable

Within-subjects design

Dummy variable

T-test

P-P plot

Standard deviation

Standard error

SPSS

Effect size

Bar chart

Error bar

Grand mean

Wright

Chapter 9. Comparing two means

Mahalanobis distance	In statistics, Mahalanobis distance is a distance measure introduced by P. C. Mahalanobis in 1936. It is based on correlations between variables by which different patterns can be identified and analyzed. It gauges similarity of an unknown sample set to a known one. It differs from Euclidean distance in that it takes into account the correlations of the data set and is scale-invariant.
Coefficient	In mathematics, a Coefficient is a multiplicative factor in some term of an expression (or of a series); it is usually a number, but in any case does not involve any variables of the expression. For instance in $$7x^2 - 3xy + 1.5 + y$$ the first three terms respectively have Coefficients 7, −3, and 1.5 (in the third term there are no variables, so the Coefficient is the term itself; it is called the constant term or constant Coefficient of this expression). The final term does not have any explicitly written Coefficient, but is usually considered to have Coefficient 1, since multiplying by that factor would not change the term.
Independent variable	The terms 'dependent variable' and 'Independent variable' are used in similar but subtly different ways in mathematics and statistics as part of the standard terminology in those subjects. They are used to distinguish between two types of quantities being considered, separating them into those available at the start of a process and those being created by it, where the latter (dependent variables) are dependent on the former (Independent variables). The Independent variable is typically the variable being manipulated or changed and the dependent variable is the observed result of the Independent variable being manipulated.
Within-subjects design	Within-subjects design is an experiment in which the same group of subjects serves in more than one treatment.
Dummy variable	In statistics and econometrics, particularly in regression analysis, a dummy variable (also known as an indicator variable) is one that takes the values 0 or 1 to indicate the absence or presence of some categorical effect that may be expected to shift the outcome. For example, in econometric time series analysis, dummy variables may be used to indicate the occurrence of wars, or major strikes. It could thus be thought of as a truth value represented as a numerical value 0 or 1 (as is sometimes done in computer programming).
T-test	A t-test is any statistical hypothesis test in which the test statistic follows a Student's t distribution if the null hypothesis is true. It is most commonly applied when the test statistic would follow a normal distribution if the value of a scaling term in the test statistic were known.

P-P plot	In statistics, a P-P plot is a probability plot for assessing how closely two data sets agree, which plots the two cumulative distribution functions against each other.

The Q-Q plot is more widely used, but they are both referred to as 'the' probability plot, and are potentially confused.

A P-P plot plots two cumulative distribution functions (cdfs) against each other: given two probability distributions, with cdfs 'F' and 'G', it plots $(F(z), G(z))$ as z ranges from $-\infty$ to ∞. As a cdf has range [0,1], the domain of this parametric graph is $(-\infty, \infty)$ and the range is the unit square $[0, 1] \times [0, 1]$.

Thus for input z the output is the pair of numbers giving what percentage of f and what percentage of g fall at or below z. |
| Standard deviation | In statistics and probability theory, standard deviation shows how much variation or 'dispersion' exists from the average (mean, or expected value). A low standard deviation indicates that the data points tend to be very close to the mean; high standard deviation indicates that the data points are spread out over a large range of values.

The standard deviation of a random variable, statistical population, data set, or probability distribution is the square root of its variance. |
| Standard error | The standard error is the standard deviation of the sampling distribution of a statistic. The term may also be used to refer to an estimate of that standard deviation, derived from a particular sample used to compute the estimate.

For example, the sample mean is the usual estimator of a population mean. |
| SPSS | SPSS Statistics is a software package used for statistical analysis. It is now officially named 'IBM SPSS Statistics'. Companion products in the same family are used for survey authoring and deployment (IBM SPSS Data Collection), data mining (IBM SPSS Modeler), text analytics, and collaboration and deployment (batch and automated scoring services). |
| Effect size | In statistics, an effect size is a measure of the strength of a phenomenon (for example, the relationship between two variables in a statistical population) or a sample-based estimate of that quantity. An effect size calculated from data is a descriptive statistic that conveys the estimated magnitude of a relationship without making any statement about whether the apparent relationship in the data reflects a true relationship in the population. In that way, effect sizes complement inferential statistics such as p-values. |

Chapter 9. Comparing two means

Bar chart	A bar chart is a chart with rectangular bars with lengths proportional to the values that they represent. The bars can be plotted vertically or horizontally. A vertical bar chart is sometimes called a column bar chart.
Error bar	Error bars are a graphical representation of the variability of data and are used on graphs to indicate the error, or uncertainty in a reported measurement. They give a general idea of how accurate a measurement is, or conversely, how far from the reported value the true (error free) value might be. Error bars often represent one standard deviation of uncertainty, one standard error, or a certain confidence interval (e.g., a 95% interval).
Grand mean	The grand mean is the mean of the means of several subsamples. For example, consider several lots, each containing several items. The items from each lot are sampled for a measure of some variable and the means of the measurements from each lot are computed.
Wright	In software architecture, Wright is an architecture description language developed at Carnegie Mellon University. Wright formalizes a software architecture in terms of concepts such as components, connectors, roles, and ports. The dynamic behavior of different ports of an individual component is described using the Communicating Sequential Processes (CSP) process algebra.

1. In software architecture, _____ is an architecture description language developed at Carnegie Mellon University. _____ formalizes a software architecture in terms of concepts such as components, connectors, roles, and ports. The dynamic behavior of different ports of an individual component is described using the Communicating Sequential Processes (CSP) process algebra.

   a. 1-factor
   b. Klecka's tau
   c. Limited dependent variable
   d. Wright

2. . The _____ is the standard deviation of the sampling distribution of a statistic. The term may also be used to refer to an estimate of that standard deviation, derived from a particular sample used to compute the estimate.

   For example, the sample mean is the usual estimator of a population mean.

   a. Relative variance
   b. Standard error

c. Sample standard deviation

d. Scale parameter

3. In statistics and econometrics, particularly in regression analysis, a _____ (also known as an indicator variable) is one that takes the values 0 or 1 to indicate the absence or presence of some categorical effect that may be expected to shift the outcome. For example, in econometric time series analysis, _____s may be used to indicate the occurrence of wars, or major strikes. It could thus be thought of as a truth value represented as a numerical value 0 or 1 (as is sometimes done in computer programming).

a. First-hitting-time model

b. Function approximation

c. Linear predictor function

d. Dummy variable

4. _____ is an experiment in which the same group of subjects serves in more than one treatment.

a. Within-subjects design

b. additive identity

c. affinely extended real number system

d. Aircraft design

5. In statistics, _____ is a distance measure introduced by P. C. Mahalanobis in 1936. It is based on correlations between variables by which different patterns can be identified and analyzed. It gauges similarity of an unknown sample set to a known one. It differs from Euclidean distance in that it takes into account the correlations of the data set and is scale-invariant.

a. Mahalanobis distance

b. Multidimensional scaling

c. NOMINATE

d. Preference regression

1. d
2. b
3. d
4. a
5. a

You can take the complete Chapter Practice Test

for Chapter 9. Comparing two means
on all key terms, persons, places, and concepts.

Online 99 Cents

http://www.epub27.31.21776.9.cram101.com/

Use www.Cram101.com for all your study needs

including Cram101's online interactive problem solving labs in

chemistry, statistics, mathematics, and more.

Chapter 10. Moderation, mediation and more regression

CHAPTER OUTLINE: KEY TERMS, PEOPLE, PLACES, CONCEPTS

Conceptual model

Interaction

Moderation

Moderator variable

Predictor variable

Statistical model

Grand mean

Interaction variable

SPSS

BARON

Factor analysis

Sobel test

Effect size

Dummy variable

Conceptual model	In the most general sense, a model is anything used in any way to represent anything else. Some models are physical objects, for instance, a toy model which may be assembled, and may even be made to work like the object it represents. Whereas, a conceptual model is a model that exists only in the mind.
Interaction	In statistics, an interaction may arise when considering the relationship among three or more variables, and describes a situation in which the simultaneous influence of two variables on a third is not additive. Most commonly, interactions are considered in the context of regression analyses. The presence of interactions can have important implications for the interpretation of statistical models.
Moderation	Moderation in Regression Analysis In statistics, moderation occurs when the relationship between two variables depends on a third variable. The third variable is referred to as the moderator variable or simply the moderator . The effect of a moderating variable is characterized statistically as an interaction; that is, a qualitative (e.g., sex, race, class) or quantitative (e.g., level of reward) variable that affects the direction and/or strength of the relation between dependent and independent variables.
Moderator variable	In statistics, moderation occurs when the relationship between two variables depends on a third variable. The third variable is referred to as the Moderator variable or simply the moderator. The effect of a moderating variable is characterized statistically as an interaction; that is, a qualitative (e.g., sex, race, class) or quantitative (e.g., level of reward) variable that affects the direction and/or strength of the relation between dependent and independent variables.
Predictor variable	The predictor variable is manipulated by the experimenter. By attempting to isolate all other factors, one can determine the influence of the independent variable on the dependent variable.
Statistical model	A statistical model is a formalization of relationships between variables in the form of mathematical equations. A statistical model describes how one or more random variables are related to one or more other variables. The model is statistical as the variables are not deterministically but stochastically related.
Grand mean	The grand mean is the mean of the means of several subsamples. For example, consider several lots, each containing several items. The items from each lot are sampled for a measure of some variable and the means of the measurements from each lot are computed.
Interaction variable	In statistics, an Interaction variable is a variable often used in regression analysis. It is formed by the multiplication of two independent variables.

Chapter 10. Moderation, mediation and more regression

SPSS	SPSS Statistics is a software package used for statistical analysis. It is now officially named 'IBM SPSS Statistics'. Companion products in the same family are used for survey authoring and deployment (IBM SPSS Data Collection), data mining (IBM SPSS Modeler), text analytics, and collaboration and deployment (batch and automated scoring services).
BARON	BARON is a computational system for solving nonconvex optimization problems to global optimality. Purely continuous, purely integer, and mixed-integer nonlinear problems can be solved with the software. BARON is available under the AIMMS and GAMS modeling languages on a variety of platforms.
Factor analysis	Factor analysis is a statistical method used to describe variability among observed, correlated variables in terms of a potentially lower number of unobserved variables called factors. In other words, it is possible, for example, that variations in three or four observed variables mainly reflect the variations in fewer unobserved variables. Factor analysis searches for such joint variations in response to unobserved latent variables.
Sobel test	In statistics, the Sobel test is a method of testing the significance of a mediation effect. The test is based on the work of Michael E. Sobel, a sociology professor at Columbia University in New York, NY. In mediation, the relationship between the independent variable and the dependent variable is hypothesized to be an indirect effect that exists due to the influence of a third variable (the mediator). As a result when the mediator is included in a regression analysis model with the independent variable, the effect of the independent variable is reduced and the effect of the mediator remains significant.
Effect size	In statistics, an effect size is a measure of the strength of a phenomenon (for example, the relationship between two variables in a statistical population) or a sample-based estimate of that quantity. An effect size calculated from data is a descriptive statistic that conveys the estimated magnitude of a relationship without making any statement about whether the apparent relationship in the data reflects a true relationship in the population. In that way, effect sizes complement inferential statistics such as p-values.
Dummy variable	In statistics and econometrics, particularly in regression analysis, a dummy variable (also known as an indicator variable) is one that takes the values 0 or 1 to indicate the absence or presence of some categorical effect that may be expected to shift the outcome. For example, in econometric time series analysis, dummy variables may be used to indicate the occurrence of wars, or major strikes. It could thus be thought of as a truth value represented as a numerical value 0 or 1 (as is sometimes done in computer programming).

Chapter 10. Moderation, mediation and more regression

1. The _____ is manipulated by the experimenter. By attempting to isolate all other factors, one can determine the influence of the independent variable on the dependent variable.

   a. Habitual offender
   b. Predictor variable
   c. Test panel
   d. Package testing

2. In statistics, an _____ may arise when considering the relationship among three or more variables, and describes a situation in which the simultaneous influence of two variables on a third is not additive. Most commonly, _____s are considered in the context of regression analyses.

   The presence of _____s can have important implications for the interpretation of statistical models.

   a. Adversarial collaboration
   b. Age adjustment
   c. Interaction
   d. Analysis of variance

3. The _____ is the mean of the means of several subsamples. For example, consider several lots, each containing several items. The items from each lot are sampled for a measure of some variable and the means of the measurements from each lot are computed.

   a. Grouped data
   b. Klecka's tau
   c. Limited dependent variable
   d. Grand mean

4. In the most general sense, a model is anything used in any way to represent anything else. Some models are physical objects, for instance, a toy model which may be assembled, and may even be made to work like the object it represents. Whereas, a _____ is a model that exists only in the mind.

   a. Deductive-nomological model
   b. Dehaene-Changeux model
   c. General Group Problem Solving Model
   d. Conceptual model

5. . In statistics and econometrics, particularly in regression analysis, a _____ (also known as an indicator variable) is one that takes the values 0 or 1 to indicate the absence or presence of some categorical effect that may be expected to shift the outcome. For example, in econometric time series analysis, _____s may be used to indicate the occurrence of wars, or major strikes. It could thus be thought of as a truth value represented as a numerical value 0 or 1 (as is sometimes done in computer programming).

   a. First-hitting-time model

b. Dummy variable

c. Linear predictor function

d. Marginal model

1. b
2. c
3. d
4. d
5. b

You can take the complete Chapter Practice Test

for Chapter 10. Moderation, mediation and more regression
on all key terms, persons, places, and concepts.

Online 99 Cents

http://www.epub27.31.21776.10.cram101.com/

Use www.Cram101.com for all your study needs

including Cram101's online interactive problem solving labs in

chemistry, statistics, mathematics, and more.

CHAPTER OUTLINE: KEY TERMS, PEOPLE, PLACES, CONCEPTS

ANOVA

Variance

Regression

Linear model

Total sum of squares

Residual sum of squares

Homogeneity

Homoscedastic

Normal distribution

SPSS

Levene's test

Familywise error rate

Post hoc

Orthogonal

Deviation

Cronbach's alpha

Q-Q plot

Polynomial

Trend analysis

	Bonferroni correction

	Two-tailed test

	Effect size

	Harmonic mean

	Sobel test

CHAPTER HIGHLIGHTS & NOTES: KEY TERMS, PEOPLE, PLACES, CONCEPTS

| ANOVA | In statistics, ANOVA is a collection of statistical models, and their associated procedures, in which the observed variance is partitioned into components due to different sources of variation. In its simplest form ANOVA provides a statistical test of whether or not the means of several groups are all equal, and therefore generalizes Student's two-sample t-test to more than two groups. ANOVAs are helpful because they possess a certain advantage over a two-sample t-test. Doing multiple two-sample t-tests would result in a largely increased chance of committing a type I error. For this reason, ANOVAs are useful in comparing three or more means.

There are three conceptual classes of such models:

· Fixed-effects models assume that the data came from normal populations which may differ only in their means. (Model 1) · Random effects models assume that the data describe a hierarchy of different populations whose differences are constrained by the hierarchy. (Model 2) · Mixed-effect models describe the situations where both fixed and random effects are present. (Model 3) |
|---|---|
| Variance | In probability theory and statistics, the variance is a measure of how far a set of numbers is spread out. It is one of several descriptors of a probability distribution, describing how far the numbers lie from the mean (expected value). In particular, the variance is one of the moments of a distribution. |
| Regression | Regression in medicine is a characteristic of diseases to show lighter symptoms without completely disappearing. At a later point, symptoms may return. |

Linear model	In statistics, the term linear model is used in different ways according to the context. The most common occurrence is in connection with regression models and the term is often taken as synonymous with linear regression model. However, the term is also used in time series analysis with a different meaning.
Total sum of squares	In statistical data analysis the total sum of squares is a quantity that appears as part of a standard way of presenting results of such analyses. It is defined as being the sum, over all observations, of the squared differences of each observation from the overall mean. In statistical linear models, (particularly in standard regression models), the TSS is the sum of the squares of the difference of the dependent variable and its grand mean: $\sum_{i=1}^{n}\left(y_i - \bar{y}\right)^2$. Where: $\bar{y}$ is the mean.
Residual sum of squares	In statistics, the residual sum of squares is the sum of squares of residuals. It is also known as the sum of squared residuals (SSR) or the sum of squared errors of prediction (SSE). It is a measure of the discrepancy between the data and an estimation model.
Homogeneity	In statistics, homogeneity and its opposite, heterogeneity, arise in describing the properties of a dataset, or several datasets. They relate to the validity of the often convenient assumption that the statistical properties of any one part of an overall dataset are the same as any other part. In meta-analysis, which combines the data from several studies, homogeneity measures the differences or similarities between the several studies .
Homoscedastic	In statistics, a sequence or a vector of random variables is homoscedastic if all random variables in the sequence or vector have the same finite variance. This is also known as homogeneity of variance. The complementary notion is called heteroscedasticity.
Normal distribution	In probability theory, the normal distribution is a continuous probability distribution that has a bell-shaped probability density function, known as the Gaussian function or informally the bell curve: $$f\left(x;\mu,\sigma^2\right) = \frac{1}{\sigma\sqrt{2\pi}}e^{-\frac{1}{2}\left(\frac{x-\mu}{\sigma}\right)^2}$$ The parameter μ is the mean or expectation (location of the peak) and σ^2 is the variance. σ is known as the standard deviation. The distribution with μ = 0 and σ^2 = 1 is called the standard normal distribution or the unit normal distribution.
SPSS	SPSS Statistics is a software package used for statistical analysis. It is now officially named 'IBM SPSS Statistics'.

Chapter 11. Comparing several means: ANOVA (GLM 1)

Levene's test	In statistics, Levene's test is an inferential statistic used to assess the equality of variances in different samples. Some common statistical procedures assume that variances of the populations from which different samples are drawn are equal. Levene's test assesses this assumption.
Familywise error rate	In statistics, familywise error rate is the probability of making one or more false discoveries, or type I errors among all the hypotheses when performing multiple hypotheses tests. FWER definition

Suppose we have m null hypotheses, denoted by: H_1, H_2, .. H_m. Using a statistical test, each hypothesis is declared significant/non-significant. Summing the test results over H_i will give us the following table and related random variables:• m_0 is the number of true null hypotheses, an unknown parameter• $m - m_0$ is the number of true alternative hypotheses• V is the number of false positives (Type I error)• S is the number of true positives• T is the number of false negatives (Type II error)• U is the number of true negatives• R is the number of rejected null hypotheses• R is an observable random variable, while S, T, U, and V are unobservable random variables

The FWER is the probability of making even one type I error In the family,

$$FWER = \Pr(V \geq 1),$$

or equivalently, $FWER = 1 - \Pr(V = 0).$

Thus, by assuring $FWER \leq \alpha,$, the probability of making even one type I error in the family is controlled at level α

A procedure controls the FWER in the weak sense if the FWER control at level α is guaranteed only when all null hypotheses are true (i.e. when $m_0 = m$ so the global null hypothesis is true)

A procedure controls the FWER in the strong sense if the FWER control at level α is guaranteed for any configuration of true and non-true null hypotheses (including the global null hypothesis) The concept of a family

Within the statistical framework, there are several definitions for the term 'family':•First of all, a distinction must be made between exploratory data analysis and confirmatory data analysis: for exploratory analysis - the family constitutes all inferences made and those that potentially could be made, whereas in the case of confirmatory analysis, the family must include only inferences of interest specified prior to the study•Hochberg & Tamhane (1987) define 'family' as 'any collection of inferences for which it is meaningful to take into account some combined measure of error'•According to Cox (1982), a set of inferences should be regarded a family:•To take into account the selection effect due to data dredging•To ensure simultaneous correctness of a set of inferences as to guarantee a correct overall decision

To summarize, a family could best be defined by the potential selective inference that is being faced: A family is the smallest set of items of inference in an analysis, interchangeable about their meaning for the goal of research, from which selection of results for action, presentation or highlighting could be made (Benjamini).

Tukey first coined the term experimentwise error rate and 'per-experiment' error rate for the error rate that the researcher should use as a control level in a multiple hypothesis experiment.

Post hoc

Post hoc ergo propter hoc, Latin for 'after this, therefore because of this', is a logical fallacy (of the questionable cause variety) that states 'Since that event followed this one, that event must have been caused by this one.' It is often shortened to simply post hoc. It is subtly different from the fallacy cum hoc ergo propter hoc, in which two things or events occur simultaneously or the chronological ordering is insignificant or unknown, also referred to as false cause, coincidental correlation, or correlation not causation.

Post hoc is a particularly tempting error because temporal sequence appears to be integral to causality.

Orthogonal

In mathematics, two functions f and g are called orthogonal if their inner product is zero with appropriate integration boundaries.

Deviation

In mathematics and statistics, deviation is a measure of difference between the observed value and the mean. The sign of deviation (positive or negative), reports the direction of that difference (it is larger when the sign is positive, and smaller if it is negative). The magnitude of the value indicates the size of the difference.

Cronbach's alpha

Cronbach's α (alpha) is a coefficient of reliability. It is commonly used as a measure of the internal consistency or reliability of a psychometric test score for a sample of examinees.

It was first named alpha by Lee Cronbach in 1951, as he had intended to continue with further coefficients. The measure can be viewed as an extension of the Kuder-Richardson Formula 20 (KR-20), which is an equivalent measure for dichotomous items. Alpha is not robust against missing data. Several other Greek letters have been used by later researchers to designate other measures used in a similar context. Somewhat related is the average variance extracted (AVE).

Cronbach's α is defined as

$$\alpha = \frac{K}{K-1}\left(1 - \frac{\sum_{i=1}^{K}\sigma_{Y_i}^2}{\sigma_X^2}\right)$$

where K is the number of components (K-items or testlets), σ_X^2 the variance of the observed total test scores, and $\sigma_{Y_i}^2$ the variance of component i for the current sample of persons.

Alternatively, the Cronbach's α can also be defined as

$$\alpha = \frac{K\bar{c}}{(\bar{v} + (K-1)\bar{c})}$$

where K is as above, $\bar{v}$ the average variance, and $\bar{c}$ the average of all covariances between the components across the current sample of persons.

The standardized Cronbach's alpha can be defined as

$$\alpha_{\text{standardized}} = \frac{K\bar{r}}{(1 + (K-1)\bar{r})}$$

where K is as above and $\bar{r}$ the mean of the K(K − 1) / 2 non-redundant correlation coefficients (i.e., the mean of an upper triangular, or lower triangular, correlation matrix).

Q-Q plot	In statistics, a Q-Q plot is a probability plot, which is a graphical method for comparing two probability distributions by plotting their quantiles against each other. First, the set of intervals for the quantiles are chosen. A point (x,y) on the plot corresponds to one of the quantiles of the second distribution (y-coordinate) plotted against the same quantile of the first distribution (x-coordinate).
Polynomial	In mathematics, a polynomial is an expression of finite length constructed from variables (also known as indeterminates) and constants, using only the operations of addition, subtraction, multiplication, and non-negative integer exponents. For example, $x^2 - 4x + 7$ is a polynomial, but $x^2 - 4/x + 7x^{3/2}$ is not, because its second term involves division by the variable x (4/x) and because its third term contains an exponent that is not a whole number (3/2).

| Trend analysis | Trend Analysis is the practice of collecting information and attempting to spot a pattern, or trend, in the information. In some fields of study, the term 'trend analysis' has more formally defined meanings.

Although trend analysis is often used to predict future events, it could be used to estimate uncertain events in the past, such as how many ancient kings probably ruled between two dates, based on data such as the average years which other known kings reigned. |
| --- | --- |
| Bonferroni correction | In statistics, the Bonferroni correction is a method used to counteract the problem of multiple comparisons. It is considered the simplest and most conservative method to control the familywise error rate. Informal introduction

Statistical inference logic is based on rejecting the null hypotheses if the likelihood under the null hypotheses of the observed data is low. |
| Two-tailed test | The two-tailed test is a statistical test used in inference, in which a given statistical hypothesis, H_0 (the null hypothesis), will be rejected when the value of the test statistic is either sufficiently small or sufficiently large. This contrasts with a one-tailed test, in which only one of the rejection regions 'sufficiently small' or 'sufficiently large' is preselected according to the alternative hypothesis being selected, and the hypothesis is rejected only if the test statistic satisfies that criterion. Alternative names are one-sided and two-sided tests.

However, the terminology is extended to tests relating to distributions other than normal. In general a test is called two-tailed if the null hypothesis is rejected for values of the test statistic falling into either tail of its sampling distribution, and it is called one-sided or one-tailed if the null hypothesis is rejected only for values of the test statistic falling into one specified tail of its sampling distribution. For example, if the alternative hypothesis is $\mu \neq 42.5$, rejecting the null hypothesis of μ = 42.5 for small or for large values of the sample mean, the test is called 'two-tailed' or 'two-sided'. If the alternative hypothesis is μ > 1.4, rejecting the null hypothesis of $\mu \leq 1.4$ only for large values of the sample mean, it is then called 'one-tailed' or 'one-sided'.

If the distribution from which the samples are derived is considered to be normal, Gaussian, or bell-shaped, then the test is referred to as a one- or two-tailed T test. If the test is performed using the actual population mean and variance, rather than an estimate from a sample, it would be called a one- or two-tailed Z test. |
| Effect size | In statistics, an effect size is a measure of the strength of a phenomenon (for example, the relationship between two variables in a statistical population) or a sample-based estimate of that quantity. |

Chapter 11. Comparing several means: ANOVA (GLM 1)

An effect size calculated from data is a descriptive statistic that conveys the estimated magnitude of a relationship without making any statement about whether the apparent relationship in the data reflects a true relationship in the population. In that way, effect sizes complement inferential statistics such as p-values.

Harmonic mean

In mathematics, the harmonic mean is one of several kinds of average. Typically, it is appropriate for situations when the average of rates is desired.

It is the special case (M^{-1}) of the power mean.

Sobel test

In statistics, the Sobel test is a method of testing the significance of a mediation effect. The test is based on the work of Michael E. Sobel, a sociology professor at Columbia University in New York, NY. In mediation, the relationship between the independent variable and the dependent variable is hypothesized to be an indirect effect that exists due to the influence of a third variable (the mediator). As a result when the mediator is included in a regression analysis model with the independent variable, the effect of the independent variable is reduced and the effect of the mediator remains significant.

1. _____ in medicine is a characteristic of diseases to show lighter symptoms without completely disappearing. At a later point, symptoms may return. These symptoms are then called recidive.

   a. Regression
   b. Transmission coefficient
   c. Vector
   d. BioSense

2. . In probability theory, the _____ is a continuous probability distribution that has a bell-shaped probability density

$$f(x; \mu, \sigma^2) = \frac{1}{\sigma\sqrt{2\pi}} e^{-\frac{1}{2}\left(\frac{x-\mu}{\sigma}\right)^2}$$

function, known as the Gaussian function or informally the bell curve:

The parameter μ is the mean or expectation (location of the peak) and σ^2 is the variance. σ is known as the standard deviation. The distribution with $\mu = 0$ and $\sigma^2 = 1$ is called the standard _____ or the unit _____.

   a. Poisson distribution
   b. Normal distribution

c. Mixed-design analysis of variance

d. Two-tailed test

3. . In statistics, _____ is the probability of making one or more false discoveries, or type I errors among all the hypotheses when performing multiple hypotheses tests. FWER definition

Suppose we have m null hypotheses, denoted by: H_1, H_2, .. H_m.Using a statistical test, each hypothesis is declared significant/non-significant.Summing the test results over H_i will give us the following table and related random variables:• m_0 is the number of true null hypotheses, an unknown parameter• $m - m_0$ is the number of true alternative hypotheses• V is the number of false positives (Type I error)• S is the number of true positives• T is the number of false negatives (Type II error)• U is the number of true negatives• R is the number of rejected null hypotheses• R is an observable random variable, while S, T, U, and V are unobservable random variables

The FWER is the probability of making even one type I error In the family, $\mathrm{FWER} = \Pr(V \geq 1)$,

or equivalently, $\mathrm{FWER} = 1 - \Pr(V = 0)$.

Thus, by assuring $\mathrm{FWER} \leq \alpha$, , the probability of making even one type I error in the family is controlled at level α

A procedure controls the FWER in the weak sense if the FWER control at level α is guaranteed only when all null hypotheses are true (i.e. when $m_0 = m$ so the global null hypothesis is true)

A procedure controls the FWER in the strong sense if the FWER control at level α is guaranteed for any configuration of true and non-true null hypotheses (including the global null hypothesis) The concept of a family

Within the statistical framework, there are several definitions for the term 'family':•First of all, a distinction must be made between exploratory data analysis and confirmatory data analysis: for exploratory analysis - the family constitutes all inferences made and those that potentially could be made, whereas in the case of confirmatory analysis, the family must include only inferences of interest specified prior to the study•Hochberg & Tamhane (1987) define 'family' as 'any collection of inferences for which it is meaningful to take into account some combined measure of error'•According to Cox (1982), a set of inferences should be regarded a family:•To take into account the selection effect due to data dredging•To ensure simultaneous correctness of a set of inferences as to guarantee a correct overall decision

To summarize, a family could best be defined by the potential selective inference that is being faced: A family is the smallest set of items of inference in an analysis, interchangeable about their meaning for the goal of research, from which selection of results for action, presentation or highlighting could be made (Benjamini).

Tukey first coined the term experimentwise error rate and 'per-experiment' error rate for the error rate that the researcher should use as a control level in a multiple hypothesis experiment.

a. Generalized p-value
b. Familywise error rate
c. Per-comparison error rate
d. Statistical significance

4. In mathematics and statistics, _____ is a measure of difference between the observed value and the mean. The sign of _____ (positive or negative), reports the direction of that difference (it is larger when the sign is positive, and smaller if it is negative). The magnitude of the value indicates the size of the difference.

a. Failure rate
b. Deviation
c. Grand mean
d. Homogeneity

5. In statistical data analysis the _____ is a quantity that appears as part of a standard way of presenting results of such analyses. It is defined as being the sum, over all observations, of the squared differences of each observation from the overall mean.

In statistical linear models, (particularly in standard regression models), the TSS is the sum of the squares of the

$$\sum_{i=1}^{n} (y_i - \bar{y})^2 \; .$$

difference of the dependent variable and its grand mean:

Where: $\bar{y}$ is the mean.

a. Total sum of squares
b. Variable rules analysis
c. Path analysis
d. Proportional hazards models

1. a
2. b
3. b
4. b
5. a

You can take the complete Chapter Practice Test

for Chapter 11. Comparing several means: ANOVA (GLM 1)
on all key terms, persons, places, and concepts.

Online 99 Cents

http://www.epub27.31.21776.11.cram101.com/

Use www.Cram101.com for all your study needs

including Cram101's online interactive problem solving labs in

chemistry, statistics, mathematics, and more.

CHAPTER OUTLINE: KEY TERMS, PEOPLE, PLACES, CONCEPTS

Covariance

Covariate

Confounding

General linear model

Linear model

Variable

Levene's test

Homogeneity

Regression

SPSS

Post hoc

Effect size

English

Categorical data

Chapter 12. Analysis of covariance, ANCOVA (GLM 2)

Covariance	In probability theory and statistics, covariance is a measure of how much two random variables change together. If the greater values of one variable mainly correspond with the greater values of the other variable, and the same holds for the smaller values, i.e., the variables tend to show similar behavior, the covariance is positive. In the opposite case, when the greater values of one variable mainly correspond to the smaller values of the other, i.e., the variables tend to show opposite behavior, the covariance is negative.
Covariate	In statistics, a covariate is a variable that is possibly predictive of the outcome under study. A covariate may be of direct interest or it may be a confounding or interacting variable. The alternative terms explanatory variable, independent variable, or predictor, are used in a regression analysis.
Confounding	In statistics, a confounding variable (also confounding factor, hidden variable, lurking variable, a confound, or confounder) is an extraneous variable in a statistical model that correlates (positively or negatively) with both the dependent variable and the independent variable. Such a relation between two observed variables is termed a spurious relationship. In the case of risk assessments evaluating the magnitude and nature of risk to human health, it is important to control for confounding to isolate the effect of a particular hazard such as a food additive, pesticide, or new drug.
General linear model	The general linear model is a statistical linear model. It may be written as $Y = XB + U,$ where Y is a matrix with series of multivariate measurements, X is a matrix that might be a design matrix, B is a matrix containing parameters that are usually to be estimated and U is a matrix containing errors or noise. The errors are usually assumed to follow a multivariate normal distribution.
Linear model	In statistics, the term linear model is used in different ways according to the context. The most common occurrence is in connection with regression models and the term is often taken as synonymous with linear regression model. However, the term is also used in time series analysis with a different meaning.
Variable	In mathematics, a variable is a value that may change within the scope of a given problem or set of operations. In contrast, a constant is a value that remains unchanged, though often unknown or undetermined. The concepts of constants and variables are fundamental to many areas of mathematics and its applications.
Levene's test	In statistics, Levene's test is an inferential statistic used to assess the equality of variances in different samples.

	Some common statistical procedures assume that variances of the populations from which different samples are drawn are equal. Levene's test assesses this assumption.
Homogeneity	In statistics, homogeneity and its opposite, heterogeneity, arise in describing the properties of a dataset, or several datasets. They relate to the validity of the often convenient assumption that the statistical properties of any one part of an overall dataset are the same as any other part. In meta-analysis, which combines the data from several studies, homogeneity measures the differences or similarities between the several studies .
Regression	Regression in medicine is a characteristic of diseases to show lighter symptoms without completely disappearing. At a later point, symptoms may return. These symptoms are then called recidive.
SPSS	SPSS Statistics is a software package used for statistical analysis. It is now officially named 'IBM SPSS Statistics'. Companion products in the same family are used for survey authoring and deployment (IBM SPSS Data Collection), data mining (IBM SPSS Modeler), text analytics, and collaboration and deployment (batch and automated scoring services).
Post hoc	Post hoc ergo propter hoc, Latin for 'after this, therefore because of this', is a logical fallacy (of the questionable cause variety) that states 'Since that event followed this one, that event must have been caused by this one.' It is often shortened to simply post hoc. It is subtly different from the fallacy cum hoc ergo propter hoc, in which two things or events occur simultaneously or the chronological ordering is insignificant or unknown, also referred to as false cause, coincidental correlation, or correlation not causation. Post hoc is a particularly tempting error because temporal sequence appears to be integral to causality.
Effect size	In statistics, an effect size is a measure of the strength of a phenomenon (for example, the relationship between two variables in a statistical population) or a sample-based estimate of that quantity. An effect size calculated from data is a descriptive statistic that conveys the estimated magnitude of a relationship without making any statement about whether the apparent relationship in the data reflects a true relationship in the population. In that way, effect sizes complement inferential statistics such as p-values.
English	English is a database retrieval and reporting language somewhat like SQL, but with no programming or update abilities. It was originally released by Microdata in 1973 and named so that the company's brochures could claim that developers could generate reports on their implementation of the Pick operating system using English.

Chapter 12. Analysis of covariance, ANCOVA (GLM 2)

Categorical data	In statistics, categorical data is that part of an observed dataset that consists of categorical variables, or for data that has been converted into that form, for example as grouped data. More specifically, categorical data may derive from either or both of observations made of qualitative data, where the observations are summarised as counts or cross tabulations, or of quantitative data, where observations might be directly observed counts of events happening or they might counts of values that occur within given intervals. Often, purely categorical data are summarised in the form of a contingency table.

1. In probability theory and statistics, _____ is a measure of how much two random variables change together. If the greater values of one variable mainly correspond with the greater values of the other variable, and the same holds for the smaller values, i.e., the variables tend to show similar behavior, the _____ is positive. In the opposite case, when the greater values of one variable mainly correspond to the smaller values of the other, i.e., the variables tend to show opposite behavior, the _____ is negative.

   a. Covariance
   b. Law of total cumulance
   c. Law of total expectation
   d. Law of total variance

2. _____ in medicine is a characteristic of diseases to show lighter symptoms without completely disappearing. At a later point, symptoms may return. These symptoms are then called recidive.

   a. Transmission
   b. Transmission coefficient
   c. Regression
   d. BioSense

3. . In statistics, a _____ is a variable that is possibly predictive of the outcome under study. A _____ may be of direct interest or it may be a confounding or interacting variable.

   The alternative terms explanatory variable, independent variable, or predictor, are used in a regression analysis.

   a. Data binning
   b. Deflator
   c. Covariate

4. In statistics, a _____ variable (also _____ factor, hidden variable, lurking variable, a confound, or confounder) is an extraneous variable in a statistical model that correlates (positively or negatively) with both the dependent variable and the independent variable. Such a relation between two observed variables is termed a spurious relationship. In the case of risk assessments evaluating the magnitude and nature of risk to human health, it is important to control for _____ to isolate the effect of a particular hazard such as a food additive, pesticide, or new drug.

   a. Causality
   b. Confounding
   c. Correlation does not imply causation
   d. Covariation model

5. In mathematics, a _____ is a value that may change within the scope of a given problem or set of operations. In contrast, a constant is a value that remains unchanged, though often unknown or undetermined. The concepts of constants and _____s are fundamental to many areas of mathematics and its applications.

   a. Vinculum
   b. Y-intercept
   c. Multinomial probit
   d. Variable

1. a
2. c
3. c
4. b
5. d

You can take the complete Chapter Practice Test

for Chapter 12. Analysis of covariance, ANCOVA (GLM 2)
on all key terms, persons, places, and concepts.

Online 99 Cents

http://www.epub27.31.21776.12.cram101.com/

Use www.Cram101.com for all your study needs

including Cram101's online interactive problem solving labs in

chemistry, statistics, mathematics, and more.

Chapter 13. Factorial ANOVA (GLM 3)

_____ | Factorial ANOVA

_____ | Factorial design

_____ | ANOVA

_____ | Linear model

_____ | Test statistic

_____ | Two-tailed test

_____ | Interaction

_____ | Levene's test

_____ | Total sum of squares

_____ | Residual sum of squares

_____ | SPSS

_____ | Post hoc

_____ | Simple effect

_____ | Effect size

_____ | Sobel test

Factorial ANOVA	Factorial ANOVA is used when the experimenter wants to study the effects of two or more treatment variables. The most commonly used type of Factorial ANOVA is the 2^2 (read 'two by two') design, where there are two independent variables and each variable has two levels or distinct values. However, such use of ANOVA for analysis of 2^k factorial designs and fractional factorial designs is 'confusing and makes little sense'; instead it is suggested to refer the value of the effect divided by its standard error to a t-table. Factorial ANOVA can also be multi-level such as 3^3, etc. or higher order such as 2×2×2, etc.. Since the introduction of data analytic software, the utilization of higher order designs and analyses has become quite common.
Factorial design	In statistics, a full Factorial design is an experiment whose design consists of two or more factors, each with discrete possible values or 'levels', and whose experimental units take on all possible combinations of these levels across all such factors. A full Factorial design may also be called a fully crossed design. Such an experiment allows studying the effect of each factor on the response variable, as well as the effects of interactions between factors on the response variable.
ANOVA	In statistics, ANOVA is a collection of statistical models, and their associated procedures, in which the observed variance is partitioned into components due to different sources of variation. In its simplest form ANOVA provides a statistical test of whether or not the means of several groups are all equal, and therefore generalizes Student's two-sample t-test to more than two groups. ANOVAs are helpful because they possess a certain advantage over a two-sample t-test. Doing multiple two-sample t-tests would result in a largely increased chance of committing a type I error. For this reason, ANOVAs are useful in comparing three or more means.

There are three conceptual classes of such models:

· Fixed-effects models assume that the data came from normal populations which may differ only in their means. (Model 1) · Random effects models assume that the data describe a hierarchy of different populations whose differences are constrained by the hierarchy. (Model 2) · Mixed-effect models describe the situations where both fixed and random effects are present. (Model 3) |
| Linear model | In statistics, the term linear model is used in different ways according to the context. The most common occurrence is in connection with regression models and the term is often taken as synonymous with linear regression model. However, the term is also used in time series analysis with a different meaning. |
| Test statistic | In statistical hypothesis testing, a hypothesis test is typically specified in terms of a test statistic, which is a function of the sample; it is considered as a numerical summary of a set of data that reduces the data to one or a small number of values that can be used to perform a hypothesis test. |

Chapter 13. Factorial ANOVA (GLM 3)

Given a null hypothesis and a test statistic T, we can specify a 'null value' T_0 such that values of T close to T_0 present the strongest evidence in favor of the null hypothesis, whereas values of T far from T_0 present the strongest evidence against the null hypothesis. An important property of a test statistic is that we must be able to determine its sampling distribution under the null hypothesis, which allows us to calculate p-values.

Two-tailed test	The two-tailed test is a statistical test used in inference, in which a given statistical hypothesis, H_0 (the null hypothesis), will be rejected when the value of the test statistic is either sufficiently small or sufficiently large. This contrasts with a one-tailed test, in which only one of the rejection regions 'sufficiently small' or 'sufficiently large' is preselected according to the alternative hypothesis being selected, and the hypothesis is rejected only if the test statistic satisfies that criterion. Alternative names are one-sided and two-sided tests.

However, the terminology is extended to tests relating to distributions other than normal. In general a test is called two-tailed if the null hypothesis is rejected for values of the test statistic falling into either tail of its sampling distribution, and it is called one-sided or one-tailed if the null hypothesis is rejected only for values of the test statistic falling into one specified tail of its sampling distribution.

For example, if the alternative hypothesis is $\mu \neq 42.5$, rejecting the null hypothesis of μ = 42.5 for small or for large values of the sample mean, the test is called 'two-tailed' or 'two-sided'. If the alternative hypothesis is μ > 1.4, rejecting the null hypothesis of $\mu \leq 1.4$ only for large values of the sample mean, it is then called 'one-tailed' or 'one-sided'.

If the distribution from which the samples are derived is considered to be normal, Gaussian, or bell-shaped, then the test is referred to as a one- or two-tailed T test. If the test is performed using the actual population mean and variance, rather than an estimate from a sample, it would be called a one- or two-tailed Z test.

Interaction	In statistics, an interaction may arise when considering the relationship among three or more variables, and describes a situation in which the simultaneous influence of two variables on a third is not additive. Most commonly, interactions are considered in the context of regression analyses.

The presence of interactions can have important implications for the interpretation of statistical models.

Levene's test	In statistics, Levene's test is an inferential statistic used to assess the equality of variances in different samples. Some common statistical procedures assume that variances of the populations from which different samples are drawn are equal. Levene's test assesses this assumption.

Total sum of squares	In statistical data analysis the total sum of squares is a quantity that appears as part of a standard way of presenting results of such analyses. It is defined as being the sum, over all observations, of the squared differences of each observation from the overall mean. In statistical linear models, (particularly in standard regression models), the TSS is the sum of the squares of the difference of the dependent variable and its grand mean: $\sum_{i=1}^{n} (y_i - \bar{y})^2$. Where: $\bar{y}$ is the mean.
Residual sum of squares	In statistics, the residual sum of squares is the sum of squares of residuals. It is also known as the sum of squared residuals (SSR) or the sum of squared errors of prediction (SSE). It is a measure of the discrepancy between the data and an estimation model.
SPSS	SPSS Statistics is a software package used for statistical analysis. It is now officially named 'IBM SPSS Statistics'. Companion products in the same family are used for survey authoring and deployment (IBM SPSS Data Collection), data mining (IBM SPSS Modeler), text analytics, and collaboration and deployment (batch and automated scoring services).
Post hoc	Post hoc ergo propter hoc, Latin for 'after this, therefore because of this', is a logical fallacy (of the questionable cause variety) that states 'Since that event followed this one, that event must have been caused by this one.' It is often shortened to simply post hoc. It is subtly different from the fallacy cum hoc ergo propter hoc, in which two things or events occur simultaneously or the chronological ordering is insignificant or unknown, also referred to as false cause, coincidental correlation, or correlation not causation. Post hoc is a particularly tempting error because temporal sequence appears to be integral to causality.
Simple effect	A simple effect of an independent variable is the effect at a single level of another variable. Often they are computed following a significant interaction.
Effect size	In statistics, an effect size is a measure of the strength of a phenomenon (for example, the relationship between two variables in a statistical population) or a sample-based estimate of that quantity. An effect size calculated from data is a descriptive statistic that conveys the estimated magnitude of a relationship without making any statement about whether the apparent relationship in the data reflects a true relationship in the population. In that way, effect sizes complement inferential statistics such as p-values.
Sobel test	In statistics, the Sobel test is a method of testing the significance of a mediation effect.

Chapter 13. Factorial ANOVA (GLM 3)

> The test is based on the work of Michael E. Sobel, a sociology professor at Columbia University in New York, NY. In mediation, the relationship between the independent variable and the dependent variable is hypothesized to be an indirect effect that exists due to the influence of a third variable (the mediator). As a result when the mediator is included in a regression analysis model with the independent variable, the effect of the independent variable is reduced and the effect of the mediator remains significant.

CHAPTER QUIZ: KEY TERMS, PEOPLE, PLACES, CONCEPTS

1. The _____ is a statistical test used in inference, in which a given statistical hypothesis, H_0 (the null hypothesis), will be rejected when the value of the test statistic is either sufficiently small or sufficiently large. This contrasts with a one-tailed test, in which only one of the rejection regions 'sufficiently small' or 'sufficiently large' is preselected according to the alternative hypothesis being selected, and the hypothesis is rejected only if the test statistic satisfies that criterion. Alternative names are one-sided and two-sided tests.

    However, the terminology is extended to tests relating to distributions other than normal. In general a test is called two-tailed if the null hypothesis is rejected for values of the test statistic falling into either tail of its sampling distribution, and it is called one-sided or one-tailed if the null hypothesis is rejected only for values of the test statistic falling into one specified tail of its sampling distribution. For example, if the alternative hypothesis is $\mu \neq 42.5$, rejecting the null hypothesis of μ = 42.5 for small or for large values of the sample mean, the test is called 'two-tailed' or 'two-sided'. If the alternative hypothesis is μ > 1.4, rejecting the null hypothesis of $\mu \leq 1.4$ only for large values of the sample mean, it is then called 'one-tailed' or 'one-sided'.

    If the distribution from which the samples are derived is considered to be normal, Gaussian, or bell-shaped, then the test is referred to as a one- or two-tailed T test. If the test is performed using the actual population mean and variance, rather than an estimate from a sample, it would be called a one- or two-tailed Z test.

    a. Indexation of contracts
    b. Fraction of variance unexplained
    c. Group family
    d. Two-tailed test

2. . In statistics, an _____ is a measure of the strength of a phenomenon (for example, the relationship between two variables in a statistical population) or a sample-based estimate of that quantity. An _____ calculated from data is a descriptive statistic that conveys the estimated magnitude of a relationship without making any statement about whether the apparent relationship in the data reflects a true relationship in the population. In that way, _____s complement inferential statistics such as p-values.

a. Electronic common technical document
b. Effect size
c. Electronic patient-reported outcome
d. Ethics committee

3. _____ Statistics is a software package used for statistical analysis. It is now officially named 'IBM _____ Statistics'. Companion products in the same family are used for survey authoring and deployment (IBM _____ Data Collection), data mining (IBM _____ Modeler), text analytics, and collaboration and deployment (batch and automated scoring services).

a. StatCVS
b. Statgraphics
c. Statistical Solutions
d. SPSS

4. _____ is used when the experimenter wants to study the effects of two or more treatment variables. The most commonly used type of _____ is the 2^2 (read 'two by two') design, where there are two independent variables and each variable has two levels or distinct values. However, such use of ANOVA for analysis of 2^k factorial designs and fractional factorial designs is 'confusing and makes little sense'; instead it is suggested to refer the value of the effect divided by its standard error to a t-table. _____ can also be multi-level such as 3^3, etc. or higher order such as 2×2×2, etc.. Since the introduction of data analytic software, the utilization of higher order designs and analyses has become quite common.

a. Confidence distribution
b. Factorial ANOVA
c. Group family
d. Linear regression

5. . In statistics, _____ is a collection of statistical models, and their associated procedures, in which the observed variance is partitioned into components due to different sources of variation. In its simplest form _____ provides a statistical test of whether or not the means of several groups are all equal, and therefore generalizes Student's two-sample t-test to more than two groups. _____s are helpful because they possess a certain advantage over a two-sample t-test. Doing multiple two-sample t-tests would result in a largely increased chance of committing a type I error. For this reason, _____s are useful in comparing three or more means.

There are three conceptual classes of such models:

· Fixed-effects models assume that the data came from normal populations which may differ only in their means. (Model 1) · Random effects models assume that the data describe a hierarchy of different populations whose differences are constrained by the hierarchy. (Model 2) · Mixed-effect models describe the situations where both fixed and random effects are present. (Model 3)

a. Analysis of variance

b. ANOVA

c. Computer-assisted self-interviewing

d. Carryover effect

1. d
2. b
3. d
4. b
5. b

You can take the complete Chapter Practice Test

for Chapter 13. Factorial ANOVA (GLM 3)
on all key terms, persons, places, and concepts.

Online 99 Cents

http://www.epub27.31.21776.13.cram101.com/

Use www.Cram101.com for all your study needs

including Cram101's online interactive problem solving labs in

chemistry, statistics, mathematics, and more.

Chapter 14. Repeated-measures designs (GLM 4)

141

CHAPTER OUTLINE: KEY TERMS, PEOPLE, PLACES, CONCEPTS

Spearman's rank correlation coefficient

Coefficient

Sphericity

F-test

Bonferroni correction

Post hoc

Degree

Degrees of freedom

Freedom

Lower bound

Multivariate analysis

Multivariate analysis of variance

Variance

Total sum of squares

Residual sum of squares

Interaction

SPSS

Discriminant function analysis

Effect size

Visit Cram101.com for full Practice Exams

	Simple effect
	Mains
	ANOVA

Spearman's rank correlation coefficient	In statistics, Spearman's rank correlation coefficient is a non-parametric measure of statistical dependence between two variables. It assesses how well the relationship between two variables can be described using a monotonic function. If there are no repeated data values, a perfect Spearman correlation of +1 or −1 occurs when each of the variables is a perfect monotone function of the other.
Coefficient	In mathematics, a Coefficient is a multiplicative factor in some term of an expression (or of a series); it is usually a number, but in any case does not involve any variables of the expression. For instance in $7x^2 - 3xy + 1.5 + y$ the first three terms respectively have Coefficients 7, −3, and 1.5 (in the third term there are no variables, so the Coefficient is the term itself; it is called the constant term or constant Coefficient of this expression). The final term does not have any explicitly written Coefficient, but is usually considered to have Coefficient 1, since multiplying by that factor would not change the term.
Sphericity	Sphericity is a measure of how spherical (round) an object is. As such, it is a specific example of a compactness measure of a shape. Defined by Wadell in 1935, the sphericity, Ψ, of a particle is: the ratio of the surface area of a sphere (with the same volume as the given particle) to the surface area of the particle: $$\Psi = \frac{\pi^{\frac{1}{3}}(6V_p)^{\frac{2}{3}}}{A_p}$$ where V_p is volume of the particle and A_p is the surface area of the particle.

F-test	An F-test is any statistical test in which the test statistic has an F-distribution under the null hypothesis. It is most often used when comparing statistical models that have been fit to a data set, in order to identify the model that best fits the population from which the data were sampled. Exact F-tests mainly arise when the models have been fit to the data using least squares.
Bonferroni correction	In statistics, the Bonferroni correction is a method used to counteract the problem of multiple comparisons. It is considered the simplest and most conservative method to control the familywise error rate. Informal introduction

Statistical inference logic is based on rejecting the null hypotheses if the likelihood under the null hypotheses of the observed data is low. |
| Post hoc | Post hoc ergo propter hoc, Latin for 'after this, therefore because of this', is a logical fallacy (of the questionable cause variety) that states 'Since that event followed this one, that event must have been caused by this one.' It is often shortened to simply post hoc. It is subtly different from the fallacy cum hoc ergo propter hoc, in which two things or events occur simultaneously or the chronological ordering is insignificant or unknown, also referred to as false cause, coincidental correlation, or correlation not causation.

Post hoc is a particularly tempting error because temporal sequence appears to be integral to causality. |
| Degree | In mathematics, there are several meanings of degree depending on the subject.

A degree (in full, a degree of arc, arc degree, or arcdegree), usually denoted by ° (the degree symbol), is a measurement of a plane angle, representing $\frac{1}{360}$ of a turn. When that angle is with respect to a reference meridian, it indicates a location along a great circle of a sphere, such as Earth , Mars, or the celestial sphere. |
| Degrees of freedom | In statistics, the number of degrees of freedom is the number of values in the final calculation of a statistic that are free to vary.

Estimates of statistical parameters can be based upon different amounts of information or data. The number of independent pieces of information that go into the estimate of a parameter is called the degrees of freedom (df). |
| Freedom | Freedom (often referred to as the Freedom app) is a software program designed to keep a computer user away from the Internet for up to eight hours at a time. It is described as a way to 'free you from distractions, allowing you time to write, analyze, code, or create.' The program was written by Fred Stutzman, a Ph.D student at the University of North Carolina at Chapel Hill. |

Chapter 14. Repeated-measures designs (GLM 4)

Lower bound	In mathematics, especially in order theory, an upper bound of a subset S of some partially ordered set (P, ≤) is an element of P which is greater than or equal to every element of S. The term lower bound is defined dually as an element of P which is lesser than or equal to every element of S. A set with an upper bound is said to be bounded from above by that bound, a set with a lower bound is said to be bounded from below by that bound.

A subset S of a partially ordered set P may fail to have any bounds or may have many different upper and lower bounds. By transitivity, any element greater than or equal to an upper bound of S is again an upper bound of S, and any element lesser than or equal to any lower bound of S is again a lower bound of S. This leads to the consideration of least upper bounds: (or suprema) and greatest lower bounds (or infima). |
| Multivariate analysis | Multivariate analysis is based on the statistical principle of multivariate statistics, which involves observation and analysis of more than one statistical outcome variable at a time. In design and analysis, the technique is used to perform trade studies across multiple dimensions while taking into account the effects of all variables on the responses of interest.

Uses for multivariate analysis include:•Design for capability (also known as capability-based design)•Inverse design, where any variable can be treated as an independent variable•Analysis of Alternatives (AoA), the selection of concepts to fulfill a customer need•Analysis of concepts with respect to changing scenarios•Identification of critical design drivers and correlations across hierarchical levels

Multivariate analysis can be complicated by the desire to include physics-based analysis to calculate the effects of variables for a hierarchical 'system-of-systems.' Often, studies that wish to use multivariate analysis are stalled by the dimensionality of the problem. |
| Multivariate analysis of variance | Multivariate analysis of variance is a statistical test procedure for comparing multivariate (population) means of several groups. Unlike ANOVA, it uses the variance-covariance between variables in testing the statistical significance of the mean differences.

It is a generalized form of univariate analysis of variance (ANOVA). |
| Variance | In probability theory and statistics, the variance is a measure of how far a set of numbers is spread out. It is one of several descriptors of a probability distribution, describing how far the numbers lie from the mean (expected value). In particular, the variance is one of the moments of a distribution. |
| Total sum of squares | In statistical data analysis the total sum of squares is a quantity that appears as part of a standard way of presenting results of such analyses. It is defined as being the sum, over all observations, of the squared differences of each observation from the overall mean. |

In statistical linear models, (particularly in standard regression models), the TSS is the sum of the squares of the difference of the dependent variable and its grand mean: $\sum_{i=1}^{n}(y_i - \bar{y})^2$.

Where: $\bar{y}$ is the mean.

Residual sum of squares	In statistics, the residual sum of squares is the sum of squares of residuals. It is also known as the sum of squared residuals (SSR) or the sum of squared errors of prediction (SSE). It is a measure of the discrepancy between the data and an estimation model.
Interaction	In statistics, an interaction may arise when considering the relationship among three or more variables, and describes a situation in which the simultaneous influence of two variables on a third is not additive. Most commonly, interactions are considered in the context of regression analyses. The presence of interactions can have important implications for the interpretation of statistical models.
SPSS	SPSS Statistics is a software package used for statistical analysis. It is now officially named 'IBM SPSS Statistics'. Companion products in the same family are used for survey authoring and deployment (IBM SPSS Data Collection), data mining (IBM SPSS Modeler), text analytics, and collaboration and deployment (batch and automated scoring services).
Discriminant function analysis	Discriminant function analysis is a statistical analysis to predict a categorical dependent variable (called a grouping variable) by one or more continuous or binary independent variables (called predictor variables). The original dichotomous discriminant analysis was developed by Sir Ronald Fisher in 1936 It is different from an ANOVA or MANOVA, which is used to predict one (ANOVA) or multiple (MANOVA) continuous dependent variables by one or more independent categorical variables. Discriminant function analysis is useful in determining whether a set of variables is effective in predicting category membership Discriminant analysis is used when groups are known a priori (unlike in cluster analysis).
Effect size	In statistics, an effect size is a measure of the strength of a phenomenon (for example, the relationship between two variables in a statistical population) or a sample-based estimate of that quantity. An effect size calculated from data is a descriptive statistic that conveys the estimated magnitude of a relationship without making any statement about whether the apparent relationship in the data reflects a true relationship in the population.

Chapter 14. Repeated-measures designs (GLM 4)

Simple effect	A simple effect of an independent variable is the effect at a single level of another variable. Often they are computed following a significant interaction.
Mains	Mains is the general-purpose alternating current (AC) electric power supply. The term is not often used in the United States and Canada. In the US, Mains power is referred to by a variety of formal and informal names, including household power, household electricity, domestic power, wall power, line power, AC power, city power, and grid power.
ANOVA	In statistics, ANOVA is a collection of statistical models, and their associated procedures, in which the observed variance is partitioned into components due to different sources of variation. In its simplest form ANOVA provides a statistical test of whether or not the means of several groups are all equal, and therefore generalizes Student's two-sample t-test to more than two groups. ANOVAs are helpful because they possess a certain advantage over a two-sample t-test. Doing multiple two-sample t-tests would result in a largely increased chance of committing a type I error. For this reason, ANOVAs are useful in comparing three or more means.
	There are three conceptual classes of such models:
	· Fixed-effects models assume that the data came from normal populations which may differ only in their means. (Model 1) · Random effects models assume that the data describe a hierarchy of different populations whose differences are constrained by the hierarchy. (Model 2) · Mixed-effect models describe the situations where both fixed and random effects are present. (Model 3)

1. _____ is a statistical test procedure for comparing multivariate (population) means of several groups. Unlike ANOVA, it uses the variance-covariance between variables in testing the statistical significance of the mean differences.

   It is a generalized form of univariate analysis of variance (ANOVA).

   a. Newman-Keuls method
   b. Principle of marginality
   c. Random effects model
   d. Multivariate analysis of variance

2. . _____ is the general-purpose alternating current (AC) electric power supply. The term is not often used in the United States and Canada. In the US, _____ power is referred to by a variety of formal and informal names, including household power, household electricity, domestic power, wall power, line power, AC power, city power, and grid power.

a. Airfoil

b. Statistical database

c. Mains

d. Package testing

3. In statistics, _____ is a non-parametric measure of statistical dependence between two variables. It assesses how well the relationship between two variables can be described using a monotonic function. If there are no repeated data values, a perfect Spearman correlation of +1 or −1 occurs when each of the variables is a perfect monotone function of the other.

a. Van der Waerden test

b. Spearman's rank correlation coefficient

c. Binomial test

d. Chi-squared test

4. _____ is a measure of how spherical (round) an object is. As such, it is a specific example of a compactness measure of a shape. Defined by Wadell in 1935, the _____, Ψ , of a particle is: the ratio of the surface area of a

$$\Psi = \frac{\pi^{\frac{1}{3}}(6V_p)^{\frac{2}{3}}}{A_p}$$

sphere (with the same volume as the given particle) to the surface area of the particle:

where V_p is volume of the particle and A_p is the surface area of the particle.

a. Sphericity

b. 1-factor

c. 4-dimensional Euclidean space

d. Block Lanczos algorithm for nullspace of a matrix over a finite field

5. _____ ergo propter hoc, Latin for 'after this, therefore because of this', is a logical fallacy (of the questionable cause variety) that states 'Since that event followed this one, that event must have been caused by this one.' It is often shortened to simply _____. It is subtly different from the fallacy cum hoc ergo propter hoc, in which two things or events occur simultaneously or the chronological ordering is insignificant or unknown, also referred to as false cause, coincidental correlation, or correlation not causation.

_____ is a particularly tempting error because temporal sequence appears to be integral to causality.

a. 1-factor

b. Scheff's method

c. Post hoc

d. Block Lanczos algorithm for nullspace of a matrix over a finite field

1. d
2. c
3. b
4. a
5. c

You can take the complete Chapter Practice Test

for Chapter 14. Repeated-measures designs (GLM 4)
on all key terms, persons, places, and concepts.

Online 99 Cents

http://www.epub27.31.21776.14.cram101.com/

Use www.Cram101.com for all your study needs

including Cram101's online interactive problem solving labs in

chemistry, statistics, mathematics, and more.

Chapter 15. Mixed design ANOVA (GLM 5)

	Spearman's rank correlation coefficient
	Sphericity
	ANOVA
	SPSS
	Big Brother
	Frequency distribution

CHAPTER HIGHLIGHTS & NOTES: KEY TERMS, PEOPLE, PLACES, CONCEPTS

Spearman's rank correlation coefficient	In statistics, Spearman's rank correlation coefficient is a non-parametric measure of statistical dependence between two variables. It assesses how well the relationship between two variables can be described using a monotonic function. If there are no repeated data values, a perfect Spearman correlation of +1 or −1 occurs when each of the variables is a perfect monotone function of the other.
Sphericity	Sphericity is a measure of how spherical (round) an object is. As such, it is a specific example of a compactness measure of a shape. Defined by Wadell in 1935, the sphericity, Ψ, of a particle is: the ratio of the surface area of a sphere (with the same volume as the given particle) to the surface area of the particle: $$\Psi = \frac{\pi^{\frac{1}{3}}(6V_p)^{\frac{2}{3}}}{A_p}$$ where V_p is volume of the particle and A_p is the surface area of the particle.
ANOVA	In statistics, ANOVA is a collection of statistical models, and their associated procedures, in which the observed variance is partitioned into components due to different sources of variation. In its simplest form ANOVA provides a statistical test of whether or not the means of several groups are all equal, and therefore generalizes Student's two-sample t-test to more than two groups.

ANOVAs are helpful because they possess a certain advantage over a two-sample t-test. Doing multiple two-sample t-tests would result in a largely increased chance of committing a type I error. For this reason, ANOVAs are useful in comparing three or more means.

There are three conceptual classes of such models:

· Fixed-effects models assume that the data came from normal populations which may differ only in their means. (Model 1) · Random effects models assume that the data describe a hierarchy of different populations whose differences are constrained by the hierarchy. (Model 2) · Mixed-effect models describe the situations where both fixed and random effects are present. (Model 3)

SPSS	SPSS Statistics is a software package used for statistical analysis. It is now officially named 'IBM SPSS Statistics'. Companion products in the same family are used for survey authoring and deployment (IBM SPSS Data Collection), data mining (IBM SPSS Modeler), text analytics, and collaboration and deployment (batch and automated scoring services).
Big Brother	Big Brother (alias BB) is a tool for systems and network monitoring, generally used by system administrators. The advent of the dynamic web page allowed Big Brother to be one of the first monitoring systems to use the web as its user interface. Prior to this, monitoring tools were generally console based, or required graphic terminals such as X Window to operate.
Frequency distribution	In statistics, a frequency distribution is an arrangement of the values that one or more variables take in a sample. Each entry in the table contains the frequency or count of the occurrences of values within a particular group or interval, and in this way, the table summarizes the distribution of values in the sample. Univariate frequency tables

A different tabulation scheme aggregates values into bins such that each bin encompasses a range of values. |

Chapter 15. Mixed design ANOVA (GLM 5)

1. In statistics, _____ is a non-parametric measure of statistical dependence between two variables. It assesses how well the relationship between two variables can be described using a monotonic function. If there are no repeated data values, a perfect Spearman correlation of +1 or −1 occurs when each of the variables is a perfect monotone function of the other.

   a. Spearman's rank correlation coefficient
   b. Wilcoxon signed-rank test
   c. Binomial test
   d. Chi-squared test

2. _____ is a measure of how spherical (round) an object is. As such, it is a specific example of a compactness measure of a shape. Defined by Wadell in 1935, the _____, Ψ, of a particle is: the ratio of the surface area of a

$$\Psi = \frac{\pi^{\frac{1}{3}}(6V_p)^{\frac{2}{3}}}{A_p}$$

   sphere (with the same volume as the given particle) to the surface area of the particle:

   where V_p is volume of the particle and A_p is the surface area of the particle.

   a. Surface-area-to-volume ratio
   b. Sphericity
   c. 4-dimensional Euclidean space
   d. Chi-squared test

3. In statistics, _____ is a collection of statistical models, and their associated procedures, in which the observed variance is partitioned into components due to different sources of variation. In its simplest form _____ provides a statistical test of whether or not the means of several groups are all equal, and therefore generalizes Student's two-sample t-test to more than two groups. _____s are helpful because they possess a certain advantage over a two-sample t-test. Doing multiple two-sample t-tests would result in a largely increased chance of committing a type I error. For this reason, _____s are useful in comparing three or more means.

   There are three conceptual classes of such models:

   · Fixed-effects models assume that the data came from normal populations which may differ only in their means. (Model 1) · Random effects models assume that the data describe a hierarchy of different populations whose differences are constrained by the hierarchy. (Model 2) · Mixed-effect models describe the situations where both fixed and random effects are present. (Model 3)

   a. Analysis of variance
   b. Acceptable quality level
   c. axial
   d. ANOVA

4. _____ Statistics is a software package used for statistical analysis. It is now officially named 'IBM _____ Statistics'. Companion products in the same family are used for survey authoring and deployment (IBM _____ Data Collection), data mining (IBM _____ Modeler), text analytics, and collaboration and deployment (batch and automated scoring services).

a. StatCVS
b. Statgraphics
c. Statistical Solutions
d. SPSS

5. In statistics, a _____ is an arrangement of the values that one or more variables take in a sample. Each entry in the table contains the frequency or count of the occurrences of values within a particular group or interval, and in this way, the table summarizes the distribution of values in the sample. Univariate frequency tables

A different tabulation scheme aggregates values into bins such that each bin encompasses a range of values.

a. Lorenz asymmetry coefficient
b. Mean percentage error
c. Frequency distribution
d. Multiple of the median

ANSWER KEY
Chapter 15. Mixed design ANOVA (GLM 5)

1. a
2. b
3. d
4. d
5. c

You can take the complete Chapter Practice Test

for Chapter 15. Mixed design ANOVA (GLM 5)
on all key terms, persons, places, and concepts.

Online 99 Cents

http://www.epub27.31.21776.15.cram101.com/

Use www.Cram101.com for all your study needs

including Cram101's online interactive problem solving labs in

chemistry, statistics, mathematics, and more.

Chapter 16. Multivariate analysis of variance (MANOVA)

_____ | Discriminant function analysis

_____ | General linear model

_____ | Linear model

_____ | Multivariate analysis

_____ | Multivariate analysis of variance

_____ | Variance

_____ | MANOVA

_____ | Diagonal

_____ | Identity

_____ | ANOVA

_____ | Cross product

_____ | Total sum of squares

_____ | Residual sum of squares

_____ | Factor analysis

_____ | Inverse

_____ | Test statistic

_____ | English

_____ | Categorical data

_____ | Eigenvalue

	Harold Hotelling
	Covariance
	Homogeneity
	Sample size
	Bartlett's test
	SPSS
	Multiple comparisons
	Sphericity
	Descriptive statistic

CHAPTER HIGHLIGHTS & NOTES: KEY TERMS, PEOPLE, PLACES, CONCEPTS

Discriminant function analysis	Discriminant function analysis is a statistical analysis to predict a categorical dependent variable (called a grouping variable) by one or more continuous or binary independent variables (called predictor variables). The original dichotomous discriminant analysis was developed by Sir Ronald Fisher in 1936 It is different from an ANOVA or MANOVA, which is used to predict one (ANOVA) or multiple (MANOVA) continuous dependent variables by one or more independent categorical variables. Discriminant function analysis is useful in determining whether a set of variables is effective in predicting category membership Discriminant analysis is used when groups are known a priori (unlike in cluster analysis).
General linear model	The general linear model is a statistical linear model. It may be written as $Y = XB + U,$

where Y is a matrix with series of multivariate measurements, X is a matrix that might be a design matrix, B is a matrix containing parameters that are usually to be estimated and U is a matrix containing errors or noise. The errors are usually assumed to follow a multivariate normal distribution.

Linear model	In statistics, the term linear model is used in different ways according to the context. The most common occurrence is in connection with regression models and the term is often taken as synonymous with linear regression model. However, the term is also used in time series analysis with a different meaning.
Multivariate analysis	Multivariate analysis is based on the statistical principle of multivariate statistics, which involves observation and analysis of more than one statistical outcome variable at a time. In design and analysis, the technique is used to perform trade studies across multiple dimensions while taking into account the effects of all variables on the responses of interest.

Uses for multivariate analysis include:•Design for capability (also known as capability-based design)•Inverse design, where any variable can be treated as an independent variable•Analysis of Alternatives (AoA), the selection of concepts to fulfill a customer need•Analysis of concepts with respect to changing scenarios•Identification of critical design drivers and correlations across hierarchical levels

Multivariate analysis can be complicated by the desire to include physics-based analysis to calculate the effects of variables for a hierarchical 'system-of-systems.' Often, studies that wish to use multivariate analysis are stalled by the dimensionality of the problem. |
| Multivariate analysis of variance | Multivariate analysis of variance is a statistical test procedure for comparing multivariate (population) means of several groups. Unlike ANOVA, it uses the variance-covariance between variables in testing the statistical significance of the mean differences.

It is a generalized form of univariate analysis of variance (ANOVA). |
| Variance | In probability theory and statistics, the variance is a measure of how far a set of numbers is spread out. It is one of several descriptors of a probability distribution, describing how far the numbers lie from the mean (expected value). In particular, the variance is one of the moments of a distribution. |
| MANOVA | Multivariate analysis of variance (MANOVA) is a generalized form of univariate analysis of variance (ANOVA). It is used in cases where there are two or more dependent variables. |

Chapter 16. Multivariate analysis of variance (MANOVA)

Diagonal	A Diagonal is a line joining two nonconsecutive vertices of a polygon or polyhedron. Informally, any sloping line is called Diagonal. The word 'Diagonal' derives from the Greek διαγΪŽνιος , from dia- ('through', 'across') and gonia ('angle', related to gony 'knee'); it was used by both Strabo and Euclid to refer to a line connecting two vertices of a rhombus or cuboid and later adopted into Latin as diagonus .
Identity	In philosophy, identity, from Latin: identitas ('sameness'), is the relation each thing bears just to itself. The notion of identity gives rise to many philosophical problems, including the identity of indiscernibles , and questions about change and personal identity over time . It is important to distinguish the philosophical concept of identity from the more well-known notion of identity in use in psychology and the social sciences.
ANOVA	In statistics, ANOVA is a collection of statistical models, and their associated procedures, in which the observed variance is partitioned into components due to different sources of variation. In its simplest form ANOVA provides a statistical test of whether or not the means of several groups are all equal, and therefore generalizes Student's two-sample t-test to more than two groups. ANOVAs are helpful because they possess a certain advantage over a two-sample t-test. Doing multiple two-sample t-tests would result in a largely increased chance of committing a type I error. For this reason, ANOVAs are useful in comparing three or more means. There are three conceptual classes of such models: · Fixed-effects models assume that the data came from normal populations which may differ only in their means. (Model 1) · Random effects models assume that the data describe a hierarchy of different populations whose differences are constrained by the hierarchy. (Model 2) · Mixed-effect models describe the situations where both fixed and random effects are present. (Model 3)
Cross product	In mathematics, the Cross product is a binary operation on two vectors in a three-dimensional Euclidean space that results in another vector which is perpendicular to the plane containing the two input vectors. The algebra defined by the Cross product is neither commutative nor associative. It contrasts with the dot product which produces a scalar result.
Total sum of squares	In statistical data analysis the total sum of squares is a quantity that appears as part of a standard way of presenting results of such analyses. It is defined as being the sum, over all observations, of the squared differences of each observation from the overall mean. In statistical linear models, (particularly in standard regression models), the TSS is the sum of the squares of the difference of the dependent variable and its grand mean: $\sum_{i=1}^{n} (y_i - \bar{y})^2$.

Where: $\bar{y}$ is the mean.

Residual sum of squares	In statistics, the residual sum of squares is the sum of squares of residuals. It is also known as the sum of squared residuals (SSR) or the sum of squared errors of prediction (SSE). It is a measure of the discrepancy between the data and an estimation model.
Factor analysis	Factor analysis is a statistical method used to describe variability among observed, correlated variables in terms of a potentially lower number of unobserved variables called factors. In other words, it is possible, for example, that variations in three or four observed variables mainly reflect the variations in fewer unobserved variables. Factor analysis searches for such joint variations in response to unobserved latent variables.
Inverse	In many contexts in mathematics the term inverse indicates the opposite of something. This word and its derivatives are used widely in mathematics, as illustrated below. •Inverse element of an element x with respect to a binary operation * with identity element e is an element y such that x * y = y * x = e.
Test statistic	In statistical hypothesis testing, a hypothesis test is typically specified in terms of a test statistic, which is a function of the sample; it is considered as a numerical summary of a set of data that reduces the data to one or a small number of values that can be used to perform a hypothesis test. Given a null hypothesis and a test statistic T, we can specify a 'null value' T_0 such that values of T close to T_0 present the strongest evidence in favor of the null hypothesis, whereas values of T far from T_0 present the strongest evidence against the null hypothesis. An important property of a test statistic is that we must be able to determine its sampling distribution under the null hypothesis, which allows us to calculate p-values.
English	English is a database retrieval and reporting language somewhat like SQL, but with no programming or update abilities. It was originally released by Microdata in 1973 and named so that the company's brochures could claim that developers could generate reports on their implementation of the Pick operating system using English.
Categorical data	In statistics, categorical data is that part of an observed dataset that consists of categorical variables, or for data that has been converted into that form, for example as grouped data. More specifically, categorical data may derive from either or both of observations made of qualitative data, where the observations are summarised as counts or cross tabulations, or of quantitative data, where observations might be directly observed counts of events happening or they might counts of values that occur within given intervals. Often, purely categorical data are summarised in the form of a contingency table.
Eigenvalue	In mathematics, Eigenvalues, eigenvectors and eigenspaces are properties of a matrix.

	They are computed by a method described below, give important information about the matrix, and can be used in matrix factorization. They have applications in areas of applied mathematics as diverse as finance and quantum mechanics.
Harold Hotelling	Harold Hotelling was a mathematical statistician and an influential economic theorist. He was Associate Professor of Mathematics at Stanford University from 1927 until 1931, a member of the faculty of Columbia University from 1931 until 1946, and a Professor of Mathematical Statistics at the University of North Carolina at Chapel Hill from 1946 until his death. A street in Chapel Hill bears his name.
Covariance	In probability theory and statistics, covariance is a measure of how much two random variables change together. If the greater values of one variable mainly correspond with the greater values of the other variable, and the same holds for the smaller values, i.e., the variables tend to show similar behavior, the covariance is positive. In the opposite case, when the greater values of one variable mainly correspond to the smaller values of the other, i.e., the variables tend to show opposite behavior, the covariance is negative.
Homogeneity	In statistics, homogeneity and its opposite, heterogeneity, arise in describing the properties of a dataset, or several datasets. They relate to the validity of the often convenient assumption that the statistical properties of any one part of an overall dataset are the same as any other part. In meta-analysis, which combines the data from several studies, homogeneity measures the differences or similarities between the several studies .
Sample size	Sample size determination is the act of choosing the number of observations or replicates to include in a statistical sample. The sample size is an important feature of any empirical study in which the goal is to make inferences about a population from a sample. In practice, the sample size used in a study is determined based on the expense of data collection, and the need to have sufficient statistical power.
Bartlett's test	In statistics, Bartlett's test is used to test if k samples are from populations with equal variances. Equal variances across samples is called homoscedasticity or homogeneity of variances. Some statistical tests, for example the analysis of variance, assume that variances are equal across groups or samples.
SPSS	SPSS Statistics is a software package used for statistical analysis. It is now officially named 'IBM SPSS Statistics'. Companion products in the same family are used for survey authoring and deployment (IBM SPSS Data Collection), data mining (IBM SPSS Modeler), text analytics, and collaboration and deployment (batch and automated scoring services).
Multiple comparisons	In statistics, the multiple comparisons, multiplicity or multiple testing problem occurs when one considers a set of statistical inferences simultaneously.

or infer on selected parameters only, where the selection depends on the observed values. Errors in inference, including confidence intervals that fail to include their corresponding population parameters or hypothesis tests that incorrectly reject the null hypothesis are more likely to occur when one considers the set as a whole.

Sphericity

Sphericity is a measure of how spherical (round) an object is. As such, it is a specific example of a compactness measure of a shape. Defined by Wadell in 1935, the sphericity, Ψ, of a particle is: the ratio of the surface area of a sphere (with the same volume as the given particle) to the surface area of the particle:

$$\Psi = \frac{\pi^{\frac{1}{3}}(6V_p)^{\frac{2}{3}}}{A_p}$$

where V_p is volume of the particle and A_p is the surface area of the particle.

Descriptive statistic

Descriptive statistics are used to describe the main features of a collection of data in quantitative terms. Descriptive statistics are distinguished from inferential statistics (or inductive statistics), in that Descriptive statistics aim to quantitatively summarize a data set, rather than being used to support inferential statements about the population that the data are thought to represent. Even when a data analysis draws its main conclusions using inductive statistical analysis, Descriptive statistics are generally presented along with more formal analyses.

1. _____ is a measure of how spherical (round) an object is. As such, it is a specific example of a compactness measure of a shape. Defined by Wadell in 1935, the _____, Ψ , of a particle is: the ratio of the surface area of a

$$\Psi = \frac{\pi^{\frac{1}{3}}(6V_p)^{\frac{2}{3}}}{A_p}$$

sphere (with the same volume as the given particle) to the surface area of the particle:

where V_p is volume of the particle and A_p is the surface area of the particle.

a. Surface-area-to-volume ratio
b. Sphericity
c. 4-dimensional Euclidean space
d. StatPlus

2. _____ is a statistical analysis to predict a categorical dependent variable (called a grouping variable) by one or more continuous or binary independent variables (called predictor variables). The original dichotomous discriminant analysis was developed by Sir Ronald Fisher in 1936 It is different from an ANOVA or MANOVA, which is used to predict one (ANOVA) or multiple (MANOVA) continuous dependent variables by one or more independent categorical variables. _____ is useful in determining whether a set of variables is effective in predicting category membership

Discriminant analysis is used when groups are known a priori (unlike in cluster analysis).

a. analytic representation
b. Discriminant function analysis
c. Andreas Raphael Blass
d. annual percentage of rate

3. The _____ is a statistical linear model. It may be written as $\mathbf{Y = XB + U,}$

where Y is a matrix with series of multivariate measurements, X is a matrix that might be a design matrix, B is a matrix containing parameters that are usually to be estimated and U is a matrix containing errors or noise. The errors are usually assumed to follow a multivariate normal distribution.

a. General linear model
b. Generalized multidimensional scaling
c. Geodemographic segmentation
d. Growth curve

4. _____s are used to describe the main features of a collection of data in quantitative terms. _____s are distinguished from inferential statistics (or inductive statistics), in that _____s aim to quantitatively summarize a data set, rather than being used to support inferential statements about the population that the data are thought to represent. Even when a data analysis draws its main conclusions using inductive statistical analysis, _____s are generally presented along with more formal analyses.

a. standard error
b. Bogardus Social Distance Scale
c. Margin of error
d. Descriptive statistic

5. . In mathematics, the _____ is a binary operation on two vectors in a three-dimensional Euclidean space that results in another vector which is perpendicular to the plane containing the two input vectors. The algebra defined by the _____ is neither commutative nor associative. It contrasts with the dot product which produces a scalar result.

a. Cross product
b. Polarization identity
c. vector

1. b
2. b
3. a
4. d
5. a

You can take the complete Chapter Practice Test

for Chapter 16. Multivariate analysis of variance (MANOVA)
on all key terms, persons, places, and concepts.

Online 99 Cents

http://www.epub27.31.21776.16.cram101.com/

Use www.Cram101.com for all your study needs

including Cram101's online interactive problem solving labs in

chemistry, statistics, mathematics, and more.

	Factor analysis
	Frequency distribution
	Latent variable
	Principal
	Principal component
	Principal components analysis
	R-matrix
	Coefficient
	Component
	Graphic communication
	Weighted average
	Correlation
	Linear regression
	Orthogonal
	Regression coefficient
	Rotation
	Confirmatory factor analysis
	Hypothetico-deductive model
	Randomization

Chapter 17. Exploratory factor analysis
CHAPTER OUTLINE: KEY TERMS, PEOPLE, PLACES, CONCEPTS

_____ | Unique variance

_____ | Q-Q plot

_____ | Sample size

_____ | Sampling

_____ | Bartlett's test

_____ | Multicollinearity

_____ | SPSS

_____ | Distribution

_____ | Singularity

_____ | Determinant

_____ | Matrix

_____ | Variance-covariance matrix

_____ | Cronbach's alpha

_____ | Reliability

_____ | Split-half reliability

_____ | Intraclass correlation

Factor analysis	Factor analysis is a statistical method used to describe variability among observed, correlated variables in terms of a potentially lower number of unobserved variables called factors. In other words, it is possible, for example, that variations in three or four observed variables mainly reflect the variations in fewer unobserved variables. Factor analysis searches for such joint variations in response to unobserved latent variables.
Frequency distribution	In statistics, a frequency distribution is an arrangement of the values that one or more variables take in a sample. Each entry in the table contains the frequency or count of the occurrences of values within a particular group or interval, and in this way, the table summarizes the distribution of values in the sample. Univariate frequency tables A different tabulation scheme aggregates values into bins such that each bin encompasses a range of values.
Latent variable	In statistics, latent variables (as opposed to observable variables), are variables that are not directly observed but are rather inferred (through a mathematical model) from other variables that are observed (directly measured). Mathematical models that aim to explain observed variables in terms of latent variables are called latent variable models. Latent variable models are used in many disciplines, including psychology, economics, machine learningartificial intelligence, bioinformatics, natural language processing, and the social sciences.
Principal	In commercial law, a principal is a person, legal or natural, who authorizes an agent to act to create one or more legal relationships with a third party. This branch of law is called agency and relies on the common law proposition qui facit per alium, facit per se . It is a parallel concept to vicarious liability and strict liability (in which one person is held liable for the acts or omissions of another) in criminal law or torts.
Principal component	Principal component analysis (PCA) involves a mathematical procedure that transforms a number of possibly correlated variables into a smaller number of uncorrelated variables called principal components. The first principal component accounts for as much of the variability in the data as possible, and each succeeding component accounts for as much of the remaining variability as possible. Depending on the field of application, it is also named the discrete Karhunen-Loève transform (KLT), the Hotelling transform or proper orthogonal decomposition (POD).
Principal components analysis	Principal components analysis is a technique for simplifying a dataset. It is a linear transformation that transforms the data to a new coordinate system such that the greatest variance by any projection of the data comes to lie on the first coordinate, the second greatest variance on the second coordinate, and so on.

Chapter 17. Exploratory factor analysis

R-matrix	The term R-matrix has several meanings, depending on the field of study. The term R-matrix is used in connection with the Yang-Baxter equation. This is an equation which was first introduced in the field of statistical mechanics, taking its name from independent work of C. N. Yang and R. J. Baxter.
Coefficient	In mathematics, a Coefficient is a multiplicative factor in some term of an expression (or of a series); it is usually a number, but in any case does not involve any variables of the expression. For instance in $7x^2 - 3xy + 1.5 + y$ the first three terms respectively have Coefficients 7, −3, and 1.5 (in the third term there are no variables, so the Coefficient is the term itself; it is called the constant term or constant Coefficient of this expression). The final term does not have any explicitly written Coefficient, but is usually considered to have Coefficient 1, since multiplying by that factor would not change the term.
Component	A component in the Unified Modeling Language 'represents a modular part of a system, that encapsulates its content and whose manifestation is replaceable within its environment. A component defines its behavior in terms of provided and required interfaces'. A component may be replaced by another if and only if their provided and required interfaces are identical.
Graphic communication	Graphic communication as the name suggests is communication through graphics and graphical aids. It is the process of creating, producing, and distributing material incorporating words and images to convey data, concepts, and emotions. The field of Graphic communications encompasses all phases of the Graphic communications processes from origination of the idea (design, layout, and typography) through reproduction, finishing and distribution of two- or three-dimensional products or electronic transmissions.
Weighted average	In statistics, given a set of data, X = { x1, x2, ..., xn} and corresponding non-negative weights, W = { w1, w2, ..., wn} the weighted average, is calculated as: Mean = $w_i x_i$ / w_i.
Correlation	In statistics, correlation (often measured as a correlation coefficient, ρ) indicates the strength and direction of a relationship between two random variables. The commonest use refers to a linear relationship. In general statistical usage, correlation or co-relation refers to the departure of two random variables from independence.

Chapter 17. Exploratory factor analysis

Linear regression	In statistics, linear regression is an approach to modeling the relationship between a scalar dependent variable y and one or more explanatory variables denoted X. The case of one explanatory variable is called simple regression. More than one explanatory variable is multiple regression. (This in turn should be distinguished from multivariate linear regression, where multiple correlated dependent variables are predicted, rather than a single scalar variable).
Orthogonal	In mathematics, two functions f and g are called orthogonal if their inner product with appropriate integration boundaries.
Regression coefficient	The regression coefficient is the slope of the straight line that most closely relates two correlated variables.
Rotation	In geometry and linear algebra, a rotation is a transformation in a plane or in space that describes the motion of a rigid body around a fixed point. A rotation is different from a translation, which has no fixed points, and from a reflection, which 'flips' the bodies it is transforming. A rotation and the above-mentioned transformations are isometries; they leave the distance between any two points unchanged after the transformation.
Confirmatory factor analysis	In statistics, confirmatory factor analysis is a special form of factor analysis, most commonly used in social research. It is used to test whether measures of a construct are consistent with a researcher's understanding of the nature of that construct . As such, the objective of confirmatory factor analysis is to test whether the data fit a hypothesized measurement model.
Hypothetico-deductive model	The hypothetico-deductive model, first so-named by William Whewell, is a proposed description of scientific method. According to it, scientific inquiry proceeds by formulating a hypothesis in a form that could conceivably be falsified by a test on observable data. A test that could and does run contrary to predictions of the hypothesis is taken as a falsification of the hypothesis.
Randomization	Randomization is the process of making something random; this means:•Generating a random permutation of a sequence (such as when shuffling cards)•Selecting a random sample of a population (important in statistical sampling)•Allocating experimental units via random assignment to a treatment or control condition•Generating random numbers•Transforming a data stream (such as when using a scrambler in telecommunications) Randomization is not haphazard. Instead, a random process is a sequence of random variables describing a process whose outcomes do not follow a deterministic pattern, but follow an evolution described by probability distributions.

Visit Cram101.com for full Practice Exams

Chapter 17. Exploratory factor analysis

Unique variance	Unique variance is the variance of a variable which is not explained by common factors. It is composed of specific and error variance.
Q-Q plot	In statistics, a Q-Q plot is a probability plot, which is a graphical method for comparing two probability distributions by plotting their quantiles against each other. First, the set of intervals for the quantiles are chosen. A point (x,y) on the plot corresponds to one of the quantiles of the second distribution (y-coordinate) plotted against the same quantile of the first distribution (x-coordinate).
Sample size	Sample size determination is the act of choosing the number of observations or replicates to include in a statistical sample. The sample size is an important feature of any empirical study in which the goal is to make inferences about a population from a sample. In practice, the sample size used in a study is determined based on the expense of data collection, and the need to have sufficient statistical power.
Sampling	In statistics and survey methodology, sampling is concerned with the selection of a subset of individuals from within a population to estimate characteristics of the whole population. Researchers rarely survey the entire population because the cost of a census is too high. The three main advantages of sampling are that the cost is lower, data collection is faster, and since the data set is smaller it is possible to ensure homogeneity and to improve the accuracy and quality of the data.
Bartlett's test	In statistics, Bartlett's test is used to test if k samples are from populations with equal variances. Equal variances across samples is called homoscedasticity or homogeneity of variances. Some statistical tests, for example the analysis of variance, assume that variances are equal across groups or samples.
Multicollinearity	Multicollinearity is a statistical phenomenon in which two or more predictor variables in a multiple regression model are highly correlated. In this situation the coefficient estimates may change erratically in response to small changes in the model or the data. Multicollinearity does not reduce the predictive power or reliability of the model as a whole, at least within the sample data themselves; it only affects calculations regarding individual predictors.
SPSS	SPSS Statistics is a software package used for statistical analysis. It is now officially named 'IBM SPSS Statistics'. Companion products in the same family are used for survey authoring and deployment (IBM SPSS Data Collection), data mining (IBM SPSS Modeler), text analytics, and collaboration and deployment (batch and automated scoring services).

Singularity	In mathematics, a singularity is in general a point at which a given mathematical object is not defined, such as differentiability.
Determinant	In algebra, the Determinant is a special number associated with any square matrix. The fundamental geometric meaning of a Determinant is a scale factor or coefficient for measure when the matrix is regarded as a linear transformation. Thus a 2 × 2 matrix with Determinant 2 when applied to a set of points with finite area will transform those points into a set with twice the area.
Matrix	In mathematics, a matrix is a rectangular array of numbers, symbols, or expressions, arranged in rows and columns. The individual items in a matrix are called its elements or entries. An example of a matrix with 2 rows and 3 columns is $\begin{bmatrix} 1 & 9 & -13 \\ 20 & 5 & -6 \end{bmatrix}$. Matrices of the same size can be added or subtracted element by element.
Variance-covariance matrix	Variance-covariance matrix has variances in its diagonal and covariance in its off-diagnoal elements. It computes the covariance between each of the colums of a data matrix.
Cronbach's alpha	Cronbach's α (alpha) is a coefficient of reliability. It is commonly used as a measure of the internal consistency or reliability of a psychometric test score for a sample of examinees. It was first named alpha by Lee Cronbach in 1951, as he had intended to continue with further coefficients. The measure can be viewed as an extension of the Kuder-Richardson Formula 20 (KR-20), which is an equivalent measure for dichotomous items. Alpha is not robust against missing data. Several other Greek letters have been used by later researchers to designate other measures used in a similar context. Somewhat related is the average variance extracted (AVE). Cronbach's α is defined as $$\alpha = \frac{K}{K-1}\left(1 - \frac{\sum_{i=1}^{K}\sigma_{Y_i}^2}{\sigma_X^2}\right)$$ where K is the number of components (K-items or testlets), σ_X^2 the variance of the observed total test scores, and $\sigma_{Y_i}^2$ the variance of component i for the current sample of persons. Alternatively, the Cronbach's α can also be defined as $$\alpha = \frac{K\bar{c}}{(\bar{v} + (K-1)\bar{c})}$$ where K is as above, $\bar{v}$ the average variance, and

Chapter 17. Exploratory factor analysis

$\bar{c}$ the average of all covariances between the components across the current sample of persons.

The standardized Cronbach's alpha can be defined as

$$\alpha_{\text{standardized}} = \frac{K\bar{r}}{(1 + (K - 1)\bar{r})}$$

where K is as above and $\bar{r}$ the mean of the K(K − 1) / 2 non-redundant correlation coefficients (i.e., the mean of an upper triangular, or lower triangular, correlation matrix).

Reliability	In statistics, reliability refers to the consistency of a measure. A measure is said to have a high reliability if it produces consistent results under consistent conditions. For example, measurements of people's height and weight are often extremely reliable.
Split-half reliability	As the name suggests, split-half reliability is a coefficient obtained by dividing a test into halves, correlating the scores on each half, and then correcting for length (longer tests tend to be more reliable).
Intraclass correlation	In statistics, the intraclass correlation is a descriptive statistic that can be used when quantitative measurements are made on units that are organized into groups. It describes how strongly units in the same group resemble each other. While it is viewed as a type of correlation, unlike most other correlation measures it operates on data structured as groups, rather than data structured as paired observations.

CHAPTER QUIZ: KEY TERMS, PEOPLE, PLACES, CONCEPTS

---

1. _____ is a statistical method used to describe variability among observed, correlated variables in terms of a potentially lower number of unobserved variables called factors. In other words, it is possible, for example, that variations in three or four observed variables mainly reflect the variations in fewer unobserved variables. _____ searches for such joint variations in response to unobserved latent variables.

   a. Factor analysis
   b. 1-factor
   c. 4-dimensional Euclidean space
   d. Abu Mansur Abd al-Qahir ibn Tahir ibn Muhammad ibn Abdallah al-Tamimi al-Shaffi al-Baghdadi

2. . In statistics and survey methodology, _____ is concerned with the selection of a subset of individuals from within a population to estimate characteristics of the whole population.

   Researchers rarely survey the entire population because the cost of a census is too high.

The three main advantages of _____ are that the cost is lower, data collection is faster, and since the data set is smaller it is possible to ensure homogeneity and to improve the accuracy and quality of the data.

a. Scale analysis
b. Rankit
c. Regression control chart
d. Sampling

3. In mathematics, a _____ is a multiplicative factor in some term of an expression (or of a series); it is usually a number, but in any case does not involve any variables of the expression. For instance in

$$7x^2 - 3xy + 1.5 + y$$

the first three terms respectively have _____s 7, −3, and 1.5 (in the third term there are no variables, so the _____ is the term itself; it is called the constant term or constant _____ of this expression). The final term does not have any explicitly written _____, but is usually considered to have _____ 1, since multiplying by that factor would not change the term.

a. Determinant
b. Von Neumann's trace inequality
c. Coefficient
d. Block Lanczos algorithm for nullspace of a matrix over a finite field

4. _____ Statistics is a software package used for statistical analysis. It is now officially named 'IBM _____ Statistics'. Companion products in the same family are used for survey authoring and deployment (IBM _____ Data Collection), data mining (IBM _____ Modeler), text analytics, and collaboration and deployment (batch and automated scoring services).

a. SPSS
b. Statgraphics
c. Statistical Solutions
d. StatPlus

5. . In commercial law, a _____ is a person, legal or natural, who authorizes an agent to act to create one or more legal relationships with a third party. This branch of law is called agency and relies on the common law proposition qui facit per alium, facit per se .

It is a parallel concept to vicarious liability and strict liability (in which one person is held liable for the acts or omissions of another) in criminal law or torts.

a. Screening
b. Signalling
c. Policy Simulation Model

1. a
2. d
3. c
4. a
5. d

You can take the complete Chapter Practice Test

for Chapter 17. Exploratory factor analysis
on all key terms, persons, places, and concepts.

Online 99 Cents

http://www.epub27.31.21776.17.cram101.com/

Use www.Cram101.com for all your study needs

including Cram101's online interactive problem solving labs in

chemistry, statistics, mathematics, and more.

CHAPTER OUTLINE: KEY TERMS, PEOPLE, PLACES, CONCEPTS

Pearson's chi-square test

Contingency table

Continuity correction

Variable

Fisher's exact test

Coefficient

Chi-square

Regression

Saturated model

Loglinear analysis

Chi-square test

SPSS

Categorical data

Odds ratio

Raw score

Goodman and Kruskal's lambda

Effect size

Within-subjects design

Big Brother

Chapter 18. Categorical data
CHAPTER OUTLINE: KEY TERMS, PEOPLE, PLACES, CONCEPTS

| English |

| Levene's test |

| Frequency distribution |

CHAPTER HIGHLIGHTS & NOTES: KEY TERMS, PEOPLE, PLACES, CONCEPTS

Pearson's chi-square test

Pearson's chi-square test is the best-known of several chi-square tests - statistical procedures whose results are evaluated by reference to the chi-square distribution. Its properties were first investigated by Karl Pearson in 1900. In contexts where it is important to make a distinction between the test statistic and its distribution, names similar to Pearson X-squared test or statistic are used.

It tests a null hypothesis stating that the frequency distribution of certain events observed in a sample is consistent with a particular theoretical distribution.

Contingency table

In statistics, a contingency table is a type of table in a matrix format that displays the (multivariate) frequency distribution of the variables. The term contingency table was first used by Karl Pearson in 'On the Theory of Contingency and Its Relation to Association and Normal Correlation', part of the Drapers' Company Research Memoirs Biometric Series I published in 1904.

A crucial problem of multivariate statistics is finding (direct-)dependence structure underlying the variables contained in high dimensional contingency tables.

Continuity correction

In probability theory, if a random variable X has a binomial distribution with parameters n and p, i.e., X is distributed as the number of 'successes' in n independent Bernoulli trials with probability p of success on each trial, then $P(X \leq x) = P(X < x + 1)$

for any $x \in \{0, 1, 2, \ldots n\}$. If np and n(1 − p) are large (sometimes taken to mean ≥ 5), then the probability above is fairly well approximated by $P(Y \leq x + 1/2)$

Visit Cram101.com for full Practice Exams

where Y is a normally distributed random variable with the same expected value and the same variance as X, i.e., $E(Y) = np$ and $var(Y) = np(1 - p)$. This addition of 1/2 to x is a continuity correction.

Variable	In mathematics, a variable is a value that may change within the scope of a given problem or set of operations. In contrast, a constant is a value that remains unchanged, though often unknown or undetermined. The concepts of constants and variables are fundamental to many areas of mathematics and its applications.
Fisher's exact test	Fisher's exact test is a statistical significance test used in the analysis of contingency tables where sample sizes are small. It is named after its inventor, R. A. Fisher, and is one of a class of exact tests, so called because the significance of the deviation from a null hypothesis can be calculated exactly, rather than relying on an approximation that becomes exact in the limit as the sample size grows to infinity, as with many statistical tests. Fisher is said to have devised the test following a comment from Muriel Bristol, who claimed to be able to detect whether the tea or the milk was added first to her cup.
Coefficient	In mathematics, a Coefficient is a multiplicative factor in some term of an expression (or of a series); it is usually a number, but in any case does not involve any variables of the expression. For instance in $$7x^2 - 3xy + 1.5 + y$$ the first three terms respectively have Coefficients 7, −3, and 1.5 (in the third term there are no variables, so the Coefficient is the term itself; it is called the constant term or constant Coefficient of this expression). The final term does not have any explicitly written Coefficient, but is usually considered to have Coefficient 1, since multiplying by that factor would not change the term.
Chi-square	In probability theory and statistics, the chi-square distribution (also chi-squared or χ^2-distribution) is one of the most widely used theoretical probability distributions in inferential statistics, e.g., in statistical significance tests. It is useful because, under reasonable assumptions, easily calculated quantities can be proven to have distributions that approximate to the chi-square distribution if the null hypothesis is true. The best-known situations in which the chi-square distribution is used are the common chi-square tests for goodness of fit of an observed distribution to a theoretical one, and of the independence of two criteria of classification of qualitative data.
Regression	Regression in medicine is a characteristic of diseases to show lighter symptoms without completely disappearing. At a later point, symptoms may return.

Chapter 18. Categorical data

CHAPTER HIGHLIGHTS & NOTES: KEY TERMS, PEOPLE, PLACES, CONCEPTS

Saturated model	In mathematical logic, and particularly in its subfield model theory, a saturated model M is one which realizes as many complete types as may be 'reasonably expected' given its size. For example, an ultrapower model of the hyperreals is $\aleph_1$-saturated, meaning that every descending nested sequence of internal sets has a nonempty intersection, see Goldblatt (1998). Let κ be a finite or infinite cardinal number and M a model in some first-order language.
Loglinear analysis	Loglinear analysis is a technique used in statistics to examine the relationship between more than two categorical variables. The technique is used for both hypothesis testing and model building. In both these uses, models are tested to find the most parsimonious (i.e., least complex) model that best accounts for the variance in the observed frequencies.
Chi-square test	A chi-square test is any statistical hypothesis test in which the sampling distribution of the test statistic is a chi-square distribution when the null hypothesis is true, or any in which this is asymptotically true, meaning that the sampling distribution (if the null hypothesis is true) can be made to approximate a chi-square distribution as closely as desired by making the sample size large enough. Some examples of chi-squared tests where the chi-square distribution is only approximately valid:•Pearson's chi-square test, also known as the chi-square goodness-of-fit test or chi-square test for independence. When mentioned without any modifiers or without other precluding context, this test is usually understood .•Yates' chi-square test, also known as Yates' correction for continuity•Mantel-Haenszel chi-square test.•Linear-by-linear association chi-square test.•The portmanteau test in time-series analysis, testing for the presence of autocorrelation•Likelihood-ratio tests in general statistical modelling, for testing whether there is evidence of the need to move from a simple model to a more complicated one (where the simple model is nested within the complicated one). One case where the distribution of the test statistic is an exact chi-square distribution is the test that the variance of a normally-distributed population has a given value based on a sample variance.
SPSS	SPSS Statistics is a software package used for statistical analysis. It is now officially named 'IBM SPSS Statistics'. Companion products in the same family are used for survey authoring and deployment (IBM SPSS Data Collection), data mining (IBM SPSS Modeler), text analytics, and collaboration and deployment (batch and automated scoring services).
Categorical data	In statistics, categorical data is that part of an observed dataset that consists of categorical variables, or for data that has been converted into that form, for example as grouped data.

	More specifically, categorical data may derive from either or both of observations made of qualitative data, where the observations are summarised as counts or cross tabulations, or of quantitative data, where observations might be directly observed counts of events happening or they might counts of values that occur within given intervals. Often, purely categorical data are summarised in the form of a contingency table.
Odds ratio	The odds ratio is a measure of effect size, describing the strength of association or non-independence between two binary data values. It is used as a descriptive statistic, and plays an important role in logistic regression. Unlike other measures of association for paired binary data such as the relative risk, the odds ratio treats the two variables being compared symmetrically, and can be estimated using some types of non-random samples.
Raw score	In statistics and data analysis, a raw score is an original datum that has not been transformed. This may include, for example, the original result obtained by a student on a test (i.e., the number of correctly answered items) as opposed to that score after transformation to a standard score or percentile rank or the like. Often the conversion must be made to a standard score before the data can be used.
Goodman and Kruskal's lambda	In probability theory and statistics, Goodman & Kruskal's lambda (λ) is a measure of proportional reduction in error in cross tabulation analysis. For any sample with a nominal independent variable and dependent variable (or ones that can be treated nominally), it indicates the extent to which the modal categories and frequencies for each value of the independent variable differ from the overall modal category and frequency, i.e. for all values of the independent variable together. λ can be calculated with the equation $$\lambda = \frac{\varepsilon_1 - \varepsilon_2}{\varepsilon_1}.$$ where ε_1 is the overall non-modal frequency, and ε_2 is the sum of the non-modal frequencies for each value of the independent variable. Values for lambda range from zero (no association between independent and dependent variables) to one (perfect association). Weaknesses Although Goodman and Kruskal's lambda is used to calculate association between variables, it yields a value of 0 (no association) whenever two variables are in accord--that is, when the modal category is the same for all values of the independent variable, even if the modal frequencies or percentages vary.
Effect size	In statistics, an effect size is a measure of the strength of a phenomenon (for example, the relationship between two variables in a statistical population) or a sample-based estimate of that quantity.

Chapter 18. Categorical data

	An effect size calculated from data is a descriptive statistic that conveys the estimated magnitude of a relationship without making any statement about whether the apparent relationship in the data reflects a true relationship in the population. In that way, effect sizes complement inferential statistics such as p-values.
Within-subjects design	Within-subjects design is an experiment in which the same group of subjects serves in more than one treatment.
Big Brother	Big Brother (alias BB) is a tool for systems and network monitoring, generally used by system administrators. The advent of the dynamic web page allowed Big Brother to be one of the first monitoring systems to use the web as its user interface. Prior to this, monitoring tools were generally console based, or required graphic terminals such as X Window to operate.
English	English is a database retrieval and reporting language somewhat like SQL, but with no programming or update abilities. It was originally released by Microdata in 1973 and named so that the company's brochures could claim that developers could generate reports on their implementation of the Pick operating system using English.
Levene's test	In statistics, Levene's test is an inferential statistic used to assess the equality of variances in different samples. Some common statistical procedures assume that variances of the populations from which different samples are drawn are equal. Levene's test assesses this assumption.
Frequency distribution	In statistics, a frequency distribution is an arrangement of the values that one or more variables take in a sample. Each entry in the table contains the frequency or count of the occurrences of values within a particular group or interval, and in this way, the table summarizes the distribution of values in the sample. Univariate frequency tables A different tabulation scheme aggregates values into bins such that each bin encompasses a range of values.

Chapter 18. Categorical data

1. _____ is a statistical significance test used in the analysis of contingency tables where sample sizes are small. It is named after its inventor, R. A. Fisher, and is one of a class of exact tests, so called because the significance of the deviation from a null hypothesis can be calculated exactly, rather than relying on an approximation that becomes exact in the limit as the sample size grows to infinity, as with many statistical tests. Fisher is said to have devised the test following a comment from Muriel Bristol, who claimed to be able to detect whether the tea or the milk was added first to her cup.

   a. Friedman test
   b. Median test
   c. Multinomial test
   d. Fisher's exact test

2. In statistics, an _____ is a measure of the strength of a phenomenon (for example, the relationship between two variables in a statistical population) or a sample-based estimate of that quantity. An _____ calculated from data is a descriptive statistic that conveys the estimated magnitude of a relationship without making any statement about whether the apparent relationship in the data reflects a true relationship in the population. In that way, _____s complement inferential statistics such as p-values.

   a. Effect size
   b. Electronic data capture
   c. Electronic patient-reported outcome
   d. Ethics committee

3. In probability theory and statistics, the _____ distribution (also chi-squared or χ^2-distribution) is one of the most widely used theoretical probability distributions in inferential statistics, e.g., in statistical significance tests. It is useful because, under reasonable assumptions, easily calculated quantities can be proven to have distributions that approximate to the _____ distribution if the null hypothesis is true.

   The best-known situations in which the _____ distribution is used are the common _____ tests for goodness of fit of an observed distribution to a theoretical one, and of the independence of two criteria of classification of qualitative data.

   a. Chi-square
   b. Von Neumann's trace inequality
   c. Delta invariant
   d. Block Lanczos algorithm for nullspace of a matrix over a finite field

4. . _____ is a technique used in statistics to examine the relationship between more than two categorical variables. The technique is used for both hypothesis testing and model building. In both these uses, models are tested to find the most parsimonious (i.e., least complex) model that best accounts for the variance in the observed frequencies.

   a. Loglinear analysis
   b. Prescriptive Analytics
   c. Asian Pacific Math Olympiad

5. In statistics, _____ is an inferential statistic used to assess the equality of variances in different samples. Some common statistical procedures assume that variances of the populations from which different samples are drawn are equal. _____ assesses this assumption.

    a. Logrank test
    b. Levene's test
    c. Normality test
    d. Page's trend test

1. d
2. a
3. a
4. a
5. b

You can take the complete Chapter Practice Test

for Chapter 18. Categorical data
on all key terms, persons, places, and concepts.

Online 99 Cents

http://www.epub27.31.21776.18.cram101.com/

Use www.Cram101.com for all your study needs

including Cram101's online interactive problem solving labs in

chemistry, statistics, mathematics, and more.

CHAPTER OUTLINE: KEY TERMS, PEOPLE, PLACES, CONCEPTS

Big Brother

Linear model

Logistic regression

Chi-square

Continuity correction

Odds ratio

Hypothetico-deductive model

Block

Factor analysis

Overdispersion

English

Categorical data

Regression

Residual

Effect size

Logit

Multicollinearity

SPSS

Sobel test

Chapter 19. Logistic regression

Big Brother	Big Brother (alias BB) is a tool for systems and network monitoring, generally used by system administrators. The advent of the dynamic web page allowed Big Brother to be one of the first monitoring systems to use the web as its user interface. Prior to this, monitoring tools were generally console based, or required graphic terminals such as X Window to operate.
Linear model	In statistics, the term linear model is used in different ways according to the context. The most common occurrence is in connection with regression models and the term is often taken as synonymous with linear regression model. However, the term is also used in time series analysis with a different meaning.
Logistic regression	In statistics, logistic regression is a type of regression analysis used for predicting the outcome of a categorical (a variable that can take on a limited number of categories) dependent variable based on one or more predictor variables. The probabilities describing the possible outcome of a single trial are modelled, as a function of explanatory variables, using a logistic function.
	Logistic regression measures the relationship between a categorical dependent variable and usually a continuous independent variable, by converting the dependent variable to probability scores.
Chi-square	In probability theory and statistics, the chi-square distribution (also chi-squared or χ^2-distribution) is one of the most widely used theoretical probability distributions in inferential statistics, e.g., in statistical significance tests. It is useful because, under reasonable assumptions, easily calculated quantities can be proven to have distributions that approximate to the chi-square distribution if the null hypothesis is true.
	The best-known situations in which the chi-square distribution is used are the common chi-square tests for goodness of fit of an observed distribution to a theoretical one, and of the independence of two criteria of classification of qualitative data.
Continuity correction	In probability theory, if a random variable X has a binomial distribution with parameters n and p, i.e., X is distributed as the number of 'successes' in n independent Bernoulli trials with probability p of success on each trial, then $P(X \le x) = P(X < x + 1)$
	for any x ∈ {0, 1, 2, ... n}. If np and n(1 − p) are large (sometimes taken to mean ≥ 5), then the probability above is fairly well approximated by $P(Y \le x + 1/2)$
	where Y is a normally distributed random variable with the same expected value and the same variance as X, i.e., E(Y) = np and var(Y) = np(1 − p). This addition of 1/2 to x is a continuity correction.

Odds ratio	The odds ratio is a measure of effect size, describing the strength of association or non-independence between two binary data values. It is used as a descriptive statistic, and plays an important role in logistic regression. Unlike other measures of association for paired binary data such as the relative risk, the odds ratio treats the two variables being compared symmetrically, and can be estimated using some types of non-random samples.
Hypothetico-deductive model	The hypothetico-deductive model, first so-named by William Whewell, is a proposed description of scientific method. According to it, scientific inquiry proceeds by formulating a hypothesis in a form that could conceivably be falsified by a test on observable data. A test that could and does run contrary to predictions of the hypothesis is taken as a falsification of the hypothesis.
Block	In telecommunications a block is one of:•A group of bits or digits that is transmitted as a unit and that may be encoded for error-control purposes.•A string of records, words, or characters, that for technical or logical purposes are treated as a unit. Blocks (a) are separated by interblock gaps, (b) are delimited by an end-of-block signal, and (c) may contain one or more records. A block is usually subjected to some type of block processing, such as multidimensional parity checking, associated with it.

A block transfer attempt is a coordinated sequence of user and telecommunication system activities undertaken to effect transfer of an individual block from a source user to a destination user. |
| Factor analysis | Factor analysis is a statistical method used to describe variability among observed, correlated variables in terms of a potentially lower number of unobserved variables called factors. In other words, it is possible, for example, that variations in three or four observed variables mainly reflect the variations in fewer unobserved variables. Factor analysis searches for such joint variations in response to unobserved latent variables. |
| Overdispersion | In statistics, overdispersion is the presence of greater variability (statistical dispersion) in a data set than would be expected based on a given simple statistical model.

A common task in applied statistics is choosing a parametric model to fit a given set of empirical observations. This necessitates an assessment of the fit of the chosen model. |
| English | English is a database retrieval and reporting language somewhat like SQL, but with no programming or update abilities. It was originally released by Microdata in 1973 and named so that the company's brochures could claim that developers could generate reports on their implementation of the Pick operating system using English. |
| Categorical data | In statistics, categorical data is that part of an observed dataset that consists of categorical variables, or for data that has been converted into that form, for example as grouped data. |

Chapter 19. Logistic regression

More specifically, categorical data may derive from either or both of observations made of qualitative data, where the observations are summarised as counts or cross tabulations, or of quantitative data, where observations might be directly observed counts of events happening or they might counts of values that occur within given intervals. Often, purely categorical data are summarised in the form of a contingency table.

Regression	Regression in medicine is a characteristic of diseases to show lighter symptoms without completely disappearing. At a later point, symptoms may return. These symptoms are then called recidive.
Residual	Loosely speaking, a residual is the error in a result. To be precise, suppose we want to find x such that $f(x) = b.$ Given an approximation x_0 of x, the residual is $b - f(x_0)$ whereas the error is $x_0 - x.$ If we do not know x, we cannot compute the error but we can compute the residual. Residual of the approximation of a function Similar terminology is used dealing with differential, integral and functional equations.
Effect size	In statistics, an effect size is a measure of the strength of a phenomenon (for example, the relationship between two variables in a statistical population) or a sample-based estimate of that quantity. An effect size calculated from data is a descriptive statistic that conveys the estimated magnitude of a relationship without making any statement about whether the apparent relationship in the data reflects a true relationship in the population. In that way, effect sizes complement inferential statistics such as p-values.
Logit	The logit function is the inverse of the sigmoidal 'logistic' function used in mathematics, especially in statistics. Log-odds and logit are synonyms. The logit of a number p between 0 and 1 is given by the formula: $$\operatorname{logit}(p) = \log\left(\frac{p}{1-p}\right) = \log(p) - \log(1-p).$$

Chapter 19. Logistic regression

Multicollinearity	Multicollinearity is a statistical phenomenon in which two or more predictor variables in a multiple regression model are highly correlated. In this situation the coefficient estimates may change erratically in response to small changes in the model or the data. Multicollinearity does not reduce the predictive power or reliability of the model as a whole, at least within the sample data themselves; it only affects calculations regarding individual predictors.
SPSS	SPSS Statistics is a software package used for statistical analysis. It is now officially named 'IBM SPSS Statistics'. Companion products in the same family are used for survey authoring and deployment (IBM SPSS Data Collection), data mining (IBM SPSS Modeler), text analytics, and collaboration and deployment (batch and automated scoring services).
Sobel test	In statistics, the Sobel test is a method of testing the significance of a mediation effect. The test is based on the work of Michael E. Sobel, a sociology professor at Columbia University in New York, NY. In mediation, the relationship between the independent variable and the dependent variable is hypothesized to be an indirect effect that exists due to the influence of a third variable (the mediator). As a result when the mediator is included in a regression analysis model with the independent variable, the effect of the independent variable is reduced and the effect of the mediator remains significant.

1. The _____ is a measure of effect size, describing the strength of association or non-independence between two binary data values. It is used as a descriptive statistic, and plays an important role in logistic regression. Unlike other measures of association for paired binary data such as the relative risk, the _____ treats the two variables being compared symmetrically, and can be estimated using some types of non-random samples.

    a. Abu Mansur Abd al-Qahir ibn Tahir ibn Muhammad ibn Abdallah al-Tamimi al-Shaffi al-Baghdadi
    b. Markov chain Monte Carlo
    c. Particle filter
    d. Odds ratio

2. . _____ (alias BB) is a tool for systems and network monitoring, generally used by system administrators. The advent of the dynamic web page allowed _____ to be one of the first monitoring systems to use the web as its user interface. Prior to this, monitoring tools were generally console based, or required graphic terminals such as X Window to operate.

    a. Cacti
    b. CONFER
    c. Distributed File System

Chapter 19. Logistic regression

3. The _____, first so-named by William Whewell, is a proposed description of scientific method. According to it, scientific inquiry proceeds by formulating a hypothesis in a form that could conceivably be falsified by a test on observable data. A test that could and does run contrary to predictions of the hypothesis is taken as a falsification of the hypothesis.

    a. Jadad scale
    b. Mature technology
    c. Hypothetico-deductive model
    d. Multiple discovery

4. In statistics, the term _____ is used in different ways according to the context. The most common occurrence is in connection with regression models and the term is often taken as synonymous with linear regression model. However, the term is also used in time series analysis with a different meaning.

    a. Linear model
    b. Multicollinearity
    c. Multinomial probit
    d. Multiple correlation

5. In statistics, _____ is a type of regression analysis used for predicting the outcome of a categorical (a variable that can take on a limited number of categories) dependent variable based on one or more predictor variables. The probabilities describing the possible outcome of a single trial are modelled, as a function of explanatory variables, using a logistic function.

    _____ measures the relationship between a categorical dependent variable and usually a continuous independent variable, by converting the dependent variable to probability scores.

    a. Logit
    b. McNemar's test
    c. Multinomial test
    d. Logistic regression

ANSWER KEY
Chapter 19. Logistic regression

1. d
2. d
3. c
4. a
5. d

You can take the complete Chapter Practice Test

for Chapter 19. Logistic regression
on all key terms, persons, places, and concepts.

Online 99 Cents

http://www.epub27.31.21776.19.cram101.com/

Use www.Cram101.com for all your study needs

including Cram101's online interactive problem solving labs in

chemistry, statistics, mathematics, and more.

CHAPTER OUTLINE: KEY TERMS, PEOPLE, PLACES, CONCEPTS

_____ | Variable

_____ | Factor analysis

_____ | Intraclass correlation

_____ | Correlation

_____ | Homogeneity

_____ | Linear model

_____ | Missing data

_____ | Regression

_____ | Random effects

_____ | Random variable

_____ | Diagonal

_____ | Multicollinearity

_____ | Grand mean

_____ | Sample size

_____ | ANOVA

_____ | Estimation

_____ | Analysis of covariance

_____ | Covariance

_____ | SPSS

Chapter 20. Multilevel linear models

	Interaction
	Growth curve
	Polynomial
	Daniel Kahneman
	Levene's test
	Homoscedasticity
	Multilevel model

Variable	In mathematics, a variable is a value that may change within the scope of a given problem or set of operations. In contrast, a constant is a value that remains unchanged, though often unknown or undetermined. The concepts of constants and variables are fundamental to many areas of mathematics and its applications.
Factor analysis	Factor analysis is a statistical method used to describe variability among observed, correlated variables in terms of a potentially lower number of unobserved variables called factors. In other words, it is possible, for example, that variations in three or four observed variables mainly reflect the variations in fewer unobserved variables. Factor analysis searches for such joint variations in response to unobserved latent variables.
Intraclass correlation	In statistics, the intraclass correlation is a descriptive statistic that can be used when quantitative measurements are made on units that are organized into groups. It describes how strongly units in the same group resemble each other. While it is viewed as a type of correlation, unlike most other correlation measures it operates on data structured as groups, rather than data structured as paired observations.
Correlation	In statistics, correlation (often measured as a correlation coefficient, ρ) indicates the strength and direction of a relationship between two random variables.

The commonest use refers to a linear relationship. In general statistical usage, correlation or co-relation refers to the departure of two random variables from independence.

Homogeneity	In statistics, homogeneity and its opposite, heterogeneity, arise in describing the properties of a dataset, or several datasets. They relate to the validity of the often convenient assumption that the statistical properties of any one part of an overall dataset are the same as any other part. In meta-analysis, which combines the data from several studies, homogeneity measures the differences or similarities between the several studies .
Linear model	In statistics, the term linear model is used in different ways according to the context. The most common occurrence is in connection with regression models and the term is often taken as synonymous with linear regression model. However, the term is also used in time series analysis with a different meaning.
Missing data	In statistics, missing data, occur when no data value is stored for the variable in the current observation. Missing data are a common occurrence and can have a significant effect on the conclusions that can be drawn from the data. Types of missing data

Missing data can occur because of nonresponse: no information is provided for several items or no information is provided for a whole unit. |
| Regression | Regression in medicine is a characteristic of diseases to show lighter symptoms without completely disappearing. At a later point, symptoms may return. These symptoms are then called recidive. |
| Random effects | In statistics, a random effect(s) model, also called a variance components model, is a kind of hierarchical linear model. It assumes that the dataset being analysed consists of a hierarchy of different populations whose differences relate to that hierarchy. In econometrics, random effects models are used in the analysis of hierarchical or panel data when one assumes no fixed effects (i.e. no individual effects). |
| Random variable | In probability and statistics, a random variable is subject to variations due to chance (i.e. randomness, in a mathematical sense). As opposed to other mathematical variables, a random variable conceptually does not have a single, fixed value (even if unknown); rather, it can take on a set of possible different values, each with an associated probability.

A random variable's possible values might represent the possible outcomes of a yet-to-be-performed experiment or an event that has not happened yet, or the potential values of a past experiment or event whose already-existing value is uncertain (e.g. as a result of incomplete information or imprecise measurements). |

Chapter 20. Multilevel linear models

Diagonal	A Diagonal is a line joining two nonconsecutive vertices of a polygon or polyhedron. Informally, any sloping line is called Diagonal. The word 'Diagonal' derives from the Greek διαγἸŽνιος , from dia-('through', 'across') and gonia ('angle', related to gony 'knee'); it was used by both Strabo and Euclid to refer to a line connecting two vertices of a rhombus or cuboid and later adopted into Latin as diagonus .
Multicollinearity	Multicollinearity is a statistical phenomenon in which two or more predictor variables in a multiple regression model are highly correlated. In this situation the coefficient estimates may change erratically in response to small changes in the model or the data. Multicollinearity does not reduce the predictive power or reliability of the model as a whole, at least within the sample data themselves; it only affects calculations regarding individual predictors.
Grand mean	The grand mean is the mean of the means of several subsamples. For example, consider several lots, each containing several items. The items from each lot are sampled for a measure of some variable and the means of the measurements from each lot are computed.
Sample size	Sample size determination is the act of choosing the number of observations or replicates to include in a statistical sample. The sample size is an important feature of any empirical study in which the goal is to make inferences about a population from a sample. In practice, the sample size used in a study is determined based on the expense of data collection, and the need to have sufficient statistical power.
ANOVA	In statistics, ANOVA is a collection of statistical models, and their associated procedures, in which the observed variance is partitioned into components due to different sources of variation. In its simplest form ANOVA provides a statistical test of whether or not the means of several groups are all equal, and therefore generalizes Student's two-sample t-test to more than two groups. ANOVAs are helpful because they possess a certain advantage over a two-sample t-test. Doing multiple two-sample t-tests would result in a largely increased chance of committing a type I error. For this reason, ANOVAs are useful in comparing three or more means. There are three conceptual classes of such models: · Fixed-effects models assume that the data came from normal populations which may differ only in their means. (Model 1) · Random effects models assume that the data describe a hierarchy of different populations whose differences are constrained by the hierarchy. (Model 2) · Mixed-effect models describe the situations where both fixed and random effects are present. (Model 3)
Estimation	In project management (i.e., for engineering), accurate estimates are the basis of sound project planning.

Many processes have been developed to aid engineers in making accurate estimates, such as•Analogy based estimation•Compartmentalization (i.e., breakdown of tasks)•Delphi method•Documenting estimation results•Educated assumptions•Estimating each task•Examining historical data•Identifying dependencies•Parametric estimating•Risk assessment•Structured planning

Popular estimation processes for software projects include:•Cocomo•Cosysmo•Event chain methodology•Function points•Program Evaluation and Review Technique (PERT)•Proxy Based Estimation (PROBE) (from the Personal Software Process)•The Planning Game (from Extreme Programming)•Weighted Micro Function Points (WMFP)•Wideband Delphi.

Analysis of covariance	Covariance is a measure of how much two variables change together and how strong the relationship is between them. Analysis of covariance is a general linear model which blends ANOVA and regression. ANCOVA evaluates whether population means of a dependent variable (DV) are equal across levels of a categorical independent variable (IV), while statistically controlling for the effects of other continuous variables that are not of primary interest, known as covariates (CV).
Covariance	In probability theory and statistics, covariance is a measure of how much two random variables change together. If the greater values of one variable mainly correspond with the greater values of the other variable, and the same holds for the smaller values, i.e., the variables tend to show similar behavior, the covariance is positive. In the opposite case, when the greater values of one variable mainly correspond to the smaller values of the other, i.e., the variables tend to show opposite behavior, the covariance is negative.
SPSS	SPSS Statistics is a software package used for statistical analysis. It is now officially named 'IBM SPSS Statistics'. Companion products in the same family are used for survey authoring and deployment (IBM SPSS Data Collection), data mining (IBM SPSS Modeler), text analytics, and collaboration and deployment (batch and automated scoring services).
Interaction	In statistics, an interaction may arise when considering the relationship among three or more variables, and describes a situation in which the simultaneous influence of two variables on a third is not additive. Most commonly, interactions are considered in the context of regression analyses. The presence of interactions can have important implications for the interpretation of statistical models.
Growth curve	A growth curve is an empirical model of the evolution of a quantity over time. Growth curves are widely used in biology for quantities such as population size, body height or biomass.

Chapter 20. Multilevel linear models

Polynomial	In mathematics, a polynomial is an expression of finite length constructed from variables (also known as indeterminates) and constants, using only the operations of addition, subtraction, multiplication, and non-negative integer exponents. For example, $x^2 - 4x + 7$ is a polynomial, but $x^2 - 4/x + 7x^{3/2}$ is not, because its second term involves division by the variable x (4/x) and because its third term contains an exponent that is not a whole number (3/2). The term 'polynomial' indicates a simplified algebraic form such that all polynomials are similarly simple in complexity (cf.
Daniel Kahneman	Daniel Kahneman is an Israeli American psychologist and winner of the 2002 Nobel Memorial Prize in Economic Sciences. He is notable for his work on the psychology of judgment and decision-making, behavioral economics and hedonic psychology.
	With Amos Tversky and others, Kahneman established a cognitive basis for common human errors using heuristics and biases (Kahneman & Tversky, 1973; Kahneman, Slovic & Tversky, 1982; Tversky & Kahneman, 1974), and developed prospect theory (Kahneman & Tversky, 1979).
Levene's test	In statistics, Levene's test is an inferential statistic used to assess the equality of variances in different samples. Some common statistical procedures assume that variances of the populations from which different samples are drawn are equal. Levene's test assesses this assumption.
Homoscedasticity	In statistics, a sequence or a vector of random variables is homoscedastic if all random variables in the sequence or vector have the same finite variance. This is also known as homogeneity of variance. The complementary notion is called heteroscedasticity. The spellings homoskedasticity and heteroskedasticity are also used frequently.
	The assumption of homoscedasticity simplifies mathematical and computational treatment.
Multilevel model	Multilevel models (also hierarchical linear models, nested models, mixed models, random coefficient, random-effects models, random parameter models, or split-plot designs) are statistical models of parameters that vary at more than one level. These models can be seen as generalizations of linear models (in particular, linear regression), although they can also extend to non-linear models. Although not a new idea, they have been much more popular following the growth of computing power and availability of software.

Chapter 20. Multilevel linear models

1. _____ is an Israeli American psychologist and winner of the 2002 Nobel Memorial Prize in Economic Sciences. He is notable for his work on the psychology of judgment and decision-making, behavioral economics and hedonic psychology.

   With Amos Tversky and others, Kahneman established a cognitive basis for common human errors using heuristics and biases (Kahneman & Tversky, 1973; Kahneman, Slovic & Tversky, 1982; Tversky & Kahneman, 1974), and developed prospect theory (Kahneman & Tversky, 1979).

   a. Daniel Kahneman
   b. Nobuhiro Kiyotaki
   c. Jnos Kornai
   d. Wilhelm Krelle

2. _____ is a statistical phenomenon in which two or more predictor variables in a multiple regression model are highly correlated. In this situation the coefficient estimates may change erratically in response to small changes in the model or the data. _____ does not reduce the predictive power or reliability of the model as a whole, at least within the sample data themselves; it only affects calculations regarding individual predictors.

   a. Multinomial probit
   b. Multiple correlation
   c. Multicollinearity
   d. Nonlinear regression

3. In probability and statistics, a _____ is subject to variations due to chance (i.e. randomness, in a mathematical sense). As opposed to other mathematical variables, a _____ conceptually does not have a single, fixed value (even if unknown); rather, it can take on a set of possible different values, each with an associated probability.

   A _____'s possible values might represent the possible outcomes of a yet-to-be-performed experiment or an event that has not happened yet, or the potential values of a past experiment or event whose already-existing value is uncertain (e.g. as a result of incomplete information or imprecise measurements).

   a. Recursive partitioning
   b. Random variable
   c. Sensitivity and specificity
   d. Spatial dependence

4. . In statistics, a sequence or a vector of random variables is homoscedastic if all random variables in the sequence or vector have the same finite variance. This is also known as homogeneity of variance. The complementary notion is called heteroscedasticity. The spellings homoskedasticity and heteroskedasticity are also used frequently.

   The assumption of _____ simplifies mathematical and computational treatment.

   a. Law of total variance
   b. Homoscedasticity

c. Mean absolute error

d. Mean absolute percentage error

5. _____ in medicine is a characteristic of diseases to show lighter symptoms without completely disappearing. At a later point, symptoms may return. These symptoms are then called recidive.

a. Transmission

b. Regression

c. Vector

d. BioSense

ANSWER KEY
Chapter 20. Multilevel linear models

1. a
2. c
3. b
4. b
5. b

You can take the complete Chapter Practice Test

for Chapter 20. Multilevel linear models
on all key terms, persons, places, and concepts.

Online 99 Cents

http://www.epub27.31.21776.20.cram101.com/

Use www.Cram101.com for all your study needs

including Cram101's online interactive problem solving labs in

chemistry, statistics, mathematics, and more.

CHAPTER OUTLINE: KEY TERMS, PEOPLE, PLACES, CONCEPTS

_____ | Bartlett's test ____

_____ | ANOVA _____

_____ | Autocorrelation ____

_____ | Covariance _____

_____ | Randomization ____

_____ | Variance _____

_____ | Big Brother ____

_____ | Bonferroni correction ____

_____ | Bimodal distribution ____

_____ | Binary variable ____

_____ | Boxplot ____

_____ | Categorical data ____

_____ | Central limit theorem ____

_____ | Central tendency ____

_____ | Chartjunk ____

_____ | Chi-square ____

_____ | Logistic regression ____

_____ | Cook's distance ____

_____ | Coefficient ____

Concurrent validity

Confirmatory factor analysis

Confounding

Content validity

Contingency table

Correlation

Factor analysis

T-test

Validity

Variable

Cronbach's alpha

DFFITS

Covariate

Criterion validity

Cross-validation

Degree

Degrees of freedom

Dependent variable

Deviance

| | Freedom |

| | English |

| | Bar chart |

| | Diagonal |

| | Discrete probability distributions |

| | Discriminant function analysis |

| | Dummy variable |

| | Ecological validity |

| | Effect size |

| | Error bar |

| | Experimentwise error rate |

| | Fisher's exact test |

| | Goodman and Kruskal's lambda |

| | Levene's test |

| | Familywise error rate |

| | Frequency distribution |

| | Goodness of fit |

| | Grand mean |

| | Factorial design |

Growth curve

Harmonic mean

Heteroscedasticity

Histogram

Homogeneity

Homoscedastic

Regression

Kendall's W

Kolmogorov-Smirnov test

Independent variable

Interaction

Interquartile range

Intraclass correlation

Sampling

M-estimator

Mahalanobis distance

Kurtosis

Levels of measurement

Leverage

Line chart

Linear model

Loglinear analysis

Lower bound

Lower quartile

Main effect

McNemar's test

Monte Carlo method

Least squares

Maximum likelihood

Maximum likelihood estimation

Median

Median test

Meta-analysis

Hypothetico-deductive model

Mode

Moderation

Moderator variable

Multicollinearity

Normal distribution

Sphericity

Factorial ANOVA

Multimodal distribution

Multinomial logistic regression

Multiple regression

Multivariate analysis

Multivariate analysis of variance

Ordinary least squares

Outlier

Overdispersion

Parameter

P-P plot

Precision

Semipartial correlation

Percentile

Polynomial

Post hoc

Practice effect

Q-Q plot

Density function

Linear regression

Outcome

Predictive validity

Predictor variable

Principal

Principal component

Principal components analysis

Probability density function

Probability distribution

Quantile

Random effects

Random variable

Regression coefficient

Reliability

Shapiro-Wilk test

Residual sum of squares

Residual

Rotation

Sampling distribution

Shrinkage

Sign test

Simple effect

Sobel test

Spearman's rank correlation coefficient

Singularity

Split-half reliability

Standard deviation

Standard error

Stepwise regression

T-statistic

Test statistic

Repeatability

Total sum of squares

Truncated mean

Two-tailed test

Unique variance

	Third quartile
	Mann-Whitney U
	Wilcoxon signed-rank test
	Continuity correction
	Variance inflation factor
	Critical value
	Student t distribution
	F-distribution

CHAPTER HIGHLIGHTS & NOTES: KEY TERMS, PEOPLE, PLACES, CONCEPTS

Bartlett's test	In statistics, Bartlett's test is used to test if k samples are from populations with equal variances. Equal variances across samples is called homoscedasticity or homogeneity of variances. Some statistical tests, for example the analysis of variance, assume that variances are equal across groups or samples.
ANOVA	In statistics, ANOVA is a collection of statistical models, and their associated procedures, in which the observed variance is partitioned into components due to different sources of variation. In its simplest form ANOVA provides a statistical test of whether or not the means of several groups are all equal, and therefore generalizes Student's two-sample t-test to more than two groups. ANOVAs are helpful because they possess a certain advantage over a two-sample t-test. Doing multiple two-sample t-tests would result in a largely increased chance of committing a type I error. For this reason, ANOVAs are useful in comparing three or more means.

There are three conceptual classes of such models:

· Fixed-effects models assume that the data came from normal populations which may differ only in their means. (Model 1) |

Chapter 21. Epilogue: life after discovering statistics

· Random effects models assume that the data describe a hierarchy of different populations whose differences are constrained by the hierarchy. (Model 2) · Mixed-effect models describe the situations where both fixed and random effects are present. (Model 3)

Autocorrelation	Autocorrelation is the cross-correlation of a signal with itself. Informally, it is the similarity between observations as a function of the time separation between them. It is a mathematical tool for finding repeating patterns, such as the presence of a periodic signal which has been buried under noise, or identifying the missing fundamental frequency in a signal implied by its harmonic frequencies.
Covariance	In probability theory and statistics, covariance is a measure of how much two random variables change together. If the greater values of one variable mainly correspond with the greater values of the other variable, and the same holds for the smaller values, i.e., the variables tend to show similar behavior, the covariance is positive. In the opposite case, when the greater values of one variable mainly correspond to the smaller values of the other, i.e., the variables tend to show opposite behavior, the covariance is negative.
Randomization	Randomization is the process of making something random; this means:•Generating a random permutation of a sequence (such as when shuffling cards)•Selecting a random sample of a population (important in statistical sampling)•Allocating experimental units via random assignment to a treatment or control condition•Generating random numbers•Transforming a data stream (such as when using a scrambler in telecommunications) Randomization is not haphazard. Instead, a random process is a sequence of random variables describing a process whose outcomes do not follow a deterministic pattern, but follow an evolution described by probability distributions. For example, a random sample of individuals from a population refers to a sample where every individual has a known probability of being sampled.
Variance	In probability theory and statistics, the variance is a measure of how far a set of numbers is spread out. It is one of several descriptors of a probability distribution, describing how far the numbers lie from the mean (expected value). In particular, the variance is one of the moments of a distribution.
Big Brother	Big Brother (alias BB) is a tool for systems and network monitoring, generally used by system administrators. The advent of the dynamic web page allowed Big Brother to be one of the first monitoring systems to use the web as its user interface. Prior to this, monitoring tools were generally console based, or required graphic terminals such as X Window to operate.
Bonferroni correction	In statistics, the Bonferroni correction is a method used to counteract the problem of multiple comparisons.

	It is considered the simplest and most conservative method to control the familywise error rate. Informal introduction
	Statistical inference logic is based on rejecting the null hypotheses if the likelihood under the null hypotheses of the observed data is low.
Bimodal distribution	In statistics, a bimodal distribution is a continuous probability distribution with two different modes. These appear as distinct peaks (local maxima) in the probability density function. Terminology
	When the two modes are unequal the larger mode is known as the major mode and the other as the minor mode.
Binary variable	The term binary data has various meanings in different technical fields. In general, it refers to a unit of data which can take on only two possible values, traditionally termed 0 and 1 in accordance with the binary numeral system. Related concepts in various fields are *logical value in logic, which represents the truth or falsehood of a logical proposition•Boolean value, a representation of the concepts 'true' or 'false' used to do Boolean arithmetic in logic and computer science•binary digit, a single 0 or 1 in a binary number, used to represent numbers in base 2 (the binary numeral system) In statistics
	In statistics, binary data is a statistical data type described by binary variables, which can take only two possible values.
Boxplot	In descriptive statistics, a box plot is a convenient way of graphically depicting groups of numerical data through their five-number summaries: the smallest observation (sample minimum), lower quartile (Q1), median (Q2), upper quartile (Q3), and largest observation (sample maximum). A boxplot may also indicate which observations, if any, might be considered outliers.
	boxplots can be useful to display differences between populations without making any assumptions of the underlying statistical distribution: they are non-parametric.
Categorical data	In statistics, categorical data is that part of an observed dataset that consists of categorical variables, or for data that has been converted into that form, for example as grouped data. More specifically, categorical data may derive from either or both of observations made of qualitative data, where the observations are summarised as counts or cross tabulations, or of quantitative data, where observations might be directly observed counts of events happening or they might counts of values that occur within given intervals. Often, purely categorical data are summarised in the form of a contingency table.

Chapter 21. Epilogue: life after discovering statistics

Central limit theorem	In probability theory, the central limit theorem states that, given certain conditions, the mean of a sufficiently large number of independent random variables, each with finite mean and variance, will be approximately normally distributed. The central limit theorem has a number of variants. In its common form, the random variables must be identically distributed.
Central tendency	In statistics, the term central tendency relates to the way in which quantitative data tend to cluster around some value. A measure of central tendency is any of a number of ways of specifying this 'central value'. In practical statistical analysis, the terms are often used before one has chosen even a preliminary form of analysis: thus an initial objective might be to 'choose an appropriate measure of central tendency'.
Chartjunk	Chartjunk refers to all visual elements in charts and graphs that are not necessary to comprehend the information represented on the graph, unnecessary text or inappropriately complex fontfaces, ornamented chart axes and display frames, pictures or icons within data graphs, ornamental shading and unnecessary dimensions.
Chi-square	In probability theory and statistics, the chi-square distribution (also chi-squared or χ^2-distribution) is one of the most widely used theoretical probability distributions in inferential statistics, e.g., in statistical significance tests. It is useful because, under reasonable assumptions, easily calculated quantities can be proven to have distributions that approximate to the chi-square distribution if the null hypothesis is true.
	The best-known situations in which the chi-square distribution is used are the common chi-square tests for goodness of fit of an observed distribution to a theoretical one, and of the independence of two criteria of classification of qualitative data.
Logistic regression	In statistics, logistic regression is a type of regression analysis used for predicting the outcome of a categorical (a variable that can take on a limited number of categories) dependent variable based on one or more predictor variables. The probabilities describing the possible outcome of a single trial are modelled, as a function of explanatory variables, using a logistic function.
	Logistic regression measures the relationship between a categorical dependent variable and usually a continuous independent variable, by converting the dependent variable to probability scores.
Cook's distance	In statistics, Cook's distance is a commonly used estimate of the influence of a data point when doing least squares regression analysis. In a practical ordinary least squares analysis, Cook's distance can be used in several ways: to indicate data points that are particularly worth checking for validity; to indicate regions of the design space where it would be good to be able obtain more data points.

Coefficient	In mathematics, a Coefficient is a multiplicative factor in some term of an expression (or of a series); it is usually a number, but in any case does not involve any variables of the expression. For instance in $$7x^2 - 3xy + 1.5 + y$$ the first three terms respectively have Coefficients 7, −3, and 1.5 (in the third term there are no variables, so the Coefficient is the term itself; it is called the constant term or constant Coefficient of this expression). The final term does not have any explicitly written Coefficient, but is usually considered to have Coefficient 1, since multiplying by that factor would not change the term.
Concurrent validity	Concurrent validity is a parameter used in sociology, psychology, and other psychometric or behavioral sciences. Concurrent validity is demonstrated where a test correlates well with a measure that has previously been validated. The two measures may be for the same construct, or for different, but presumably related, constructs.
Confirmatory factor analysis	In statistics, confirmatory factor analysis is a special form of factor analysis, most commonly used in social research. It is used to test whether measures of a construct are consistent with a researcher's understanding of the nature of that construct . As such, the objective of confirmatory factor analysis is to test whether the data fit a hypothesized measurement model.
Confounding	In statistics, a confounding variable (also confounding factor, hidden variable, lurking variable, a confound, or confounder) is an extraneous variable in a statistical model that correlates (positively or negatively) with both the dependent variable and the independent variable. Such a relation between two observed variables is termed a spurious relationship. In the case of risk assessments evaluating the magnitude and nature of risk to human health, it is important to control for confounding to isolate the effect of a particular hazard such as a food additive, pesticide, or new drug.
Content validity	In psychometrics, content validity refers to the extent to which a measure represents all facets of a given social construct. For example, a depression scale may lack content validity if it only assesses the affective dimension of depression but fails to take into account the behavioral dimension. An element of subjectivity exists in relation to determining content validity, which requires a degree of agreement about what a particular personality trait such as extraversion represents.
Contingency table	In statistics, a contingency table is a type of table in a matrix format that displays the (multivariate) frequency distribution of the variables. The term contingency table was first used by Karl Pearson in 'On the Theory of Contingency and Its Relation to Association and Normal Correlation', part of the Drapers' Company Research Memoirs Biometric Series I published in 1904.

Chapter 21. Epilogue: life after discovering statistics

Correlation	In statistics, correlation (often measured as a correlation coefficient, ρ) indicates the strength and direction of a relationship between two random variables. The commonest use refers to a linear relationship. In general statistical usage, correlation or co-relation refers to the departure of two random variables from independence.
Factor analysis	Factor analysis is a statistical method used to describe variability among observed, correlated variables in terms of a potentially lower number of unobserved variables called factors. In other words, it is possible, for example, that variations in three or four observed variables mainly reflect the variations in fewer unobserved variables. Factor analysis searches for such joint variations in response to unobserved latent variables.
T-test	A t-test is any statistical hypothesis test in which the test statistic follows a Student's t distribution if the null hypothesis is true. It is most commonly applied when the test statistic would follow a normal distribution if the value of a scaling term in the test statistic were known. When the scaling term is unknown and is replaced by an estimate based on the data, the test statistic (under certain conditions) follows a Student's t distribution.
Validity	In science and statistics, validity has no single agreed definition but generally refers to the extent to which a concept, conclusion or measurement is well-founded and corresponds accurately to the real world. The word 'valid' is derived from the Latin validus, meaning strong. The validity of a measurement tool (for example, a test in education) is considered to be the degree to which the tool measures what it claims to measure.
Variable	In mathematics, a variable is a value that may change within the scope of a given problem or set of operations. In contrast, a constant is a value that remains unchanged, though often unknown or undetermined. The concepts of constants and variables are fundamental to many areas of mathematics and its applications.
Cronbach's alpha	Cronbach's α (alpha) is a coefficient of reliability. It is commonly used as a measure of the internal consistency or reliability of a psychometric test score for a sample of examinees. It was first named alpha by Lee Cronbach in 1951, as he had intended to continue with further coefficients. The measure can be viewed as an extension of the Kuder-Richardson Formula 20 (KR-20), which is an equivalent measure for dichotomous items. Alpha is not robust against missing data. Several other Greek letters have been used by later researchers to designate other measures used in a similar context. Somewhat related is the average variance extracted (AVE). $$\alpha = \frac{K}{K-1}\left(1 - \frac{\sum_{i=1}^{K} \sigma_{Y_i}^2}{\sigma_X^2}\right)$$ Cronbach's α is defined as

where K is the number of components (K-items or testlets), σ_X^2 the variance of the observed total test scores, and $\sigma_{Y_i}^2$ the variance of component i for the current sample of persons.

Alternatively, the Cronbach's α can also be defined as

$$\alpha = \frac{K\bar{c}}{(\bar{v} + (K-1)\bar{c})}$$

where K is as above, $\bar{v}$ the average variance, and $\bar{c}$ the average of all covariances between the components across the current sample of persons.

The standardized Cronbach's alpha can be defined as

$$\alpha_{\text{standardized}} = \frac{K\bar{r}}{(1 + (K-1)\bar{r})}$$

where K is as above and $\bar{r}$ the mean of the K(K − 1) / 2 non-redundant correlation coefficients (i.e., the mean of an upper triangular, or lower triangular, correlation matrix).

DFFITS

DFFITS is a diagnostic meant to show how influential a point is in a statistical regression. It was proposed in 1980. It is defined as the change ('DFFIT'), in the predicted value for a point, obtained when that point is left out of the regression, 'Studentized' by dividing by the estimated standard deviation of the fit at that point:

$$DFFITS = \frac{\hat{y}_i - \widehat{y_{i(i)}}}{s_{(i)}\sqrt{h_{ii}}}$$

where $\hat{y}_i$ and $\widehat{y_{i(i)}}$ are the prediction for point i with and without point i included in the regression, $s_{(i)}$ is the standard error estimated without the point in question, and h_{ii} is the leverage for the point.

DFFITS is very similar to the externally Studentized residual, and is in fact equal to the latter times

$$\sqrt{h_{ii}/(1 - h_{ii})}$$

.

Covariate

In statistics, a covariate is a variable that is possibly predictive of the outcome under study. A covariate may be of direct interest or it may be a confounding or interacting variable.

Chapter 21. Epilogue: life after discovering statistics

Criterion validity	In psychometrics, criterion validity is a measure of how well one variable or set of variables predicts an outcome based on information from other variables, and will be achieved if a set of measures from a personality test relate to a behavioral criterion on which psychologists agree. A typical way to achieve this is in relation to the extent to which a score on a personality test can predict future performance or behavior. Another way involves correlating test scores with another established test that also measures the same personality characteristic.
Cross-validation	Cross-validation, sometimes called rotation estimation, is a technique for assessing how the results of a statistical analysis will generalize to an independent data set. It is mainly used in settings where the goal is prediction, and one wants to estimate how accurately a predictive model will perform in practice. One round of cross-validation involves partitioning a sample of data into complementary subsets, performing the analysis on one subset (called the training set), and validating the analysis on the other subset (called the validation set or testing set).
Degree	In mathematics, there are several meanings of degree depending on the subject. A degree (in full, a degree of arc, arc degree, or arcdegree), usually denoted by ° (the degree symbol), is a measurement of a plane angle, representing $\frac{1}{360}$ of a turn. When that angle is with respect to a reference meridian, it indicates a location along a great circle of a sphere, such as Earth , Mars, or the celestial sphere.
Degrees of freedom	In statistics, the number of degrees of freedom is the number of values in the final calculation of a statistic that are free to vary. Estimates of statistical parameters can be based upon different amounts of information or data. The number of independent pieces of information that go into the estimate of a parameter is called the degrees of freedom (df).
Dependent variable	The terms 'dependent variable' and 'independent variable' are used in similar but subtly different ways in mathematics and statistics as part of the standard terminology in those subjects. They are used to distinguish between two types of quantities being considered, separating them into those available at the start of a process and those being created by it, where the latter (dependent variables) are dependent on the former (independent variables). The independent variable is typically the variable being manipulated or changed and the dependent variable is the observed result of the independent variable being manipulated.
Deviance	In statistics, deviance is a quality of fit statistic for a model that is often used for statistical hypothesis testing. The deviance for a model M_0, based on a dataset y, is defined as

$$D(y) = -2\Big(\log\left(p(y|\hat{\theta}_0)\right) - \log\left(p(y|\hat{\theta}_s)\right)\Big).$$

Here $\hat{\theta}_0$ denotes the fitted values of the parameters in the model M_0, while $\hat{\theta}_s$ denotes the fitted parameters for the 'full model' : both sets of fitted values are implicitly functions of the observations y. Here the full model is a model with a parameter for every observation so that the data are fitted exactly.

Freedom	Freedom (often referred to as the Freedom app) is a software program designed to keep a computer user away from the Internet for up to eight hours at a time. It is described as a way to 'free you from distractions, allowing you time to write, analyze, code, or create.' The program was written by Fred Stutzman, a Ph.D student at the University of North Carolina at Chapel Hill. Freedom is donationware.
English	English is a database retrieval and reporting language somewhat like SQL, but with no programming or update abilities. It was originally released by Microdata in 1973 and named so that the company's brochures could claim that developers could generate reports on their implementation of the Pick operating system using English.
Bar chart	A bar chart is a chart with rectangular bars with lengths proportional to the values that they represent. The bars can be plotted vertically or horizontally. A vertical bar chart is sometimes called a column bar chart.
Diagonal	A Diagonal is a line joining two nonconsecutive vertices of a polygon or polyhedron. Informally, any sloping line is called Diagonal. The word 'Diagonal' derives from the Greek διαγĭŽνιος , from dia- ('through', 'across') and gonia ('angle', related to gony 'knee'); it was used by both Strabo and Euclid to refer to a line connecting two vertices of a rhombus or cuboid and later adopted into Latin as diagonus .
Discrete probability distributions	Discrete probability distributions arise in the mathematical description of probabilistic and statistical problems in which the values that might be observed are restricted to being within a pre-defined list of possible values. This list has either a finite number of members, or at most is countable. In probability theory, a probability distribution is called discrete if it is characterized by a probability mass function.
Discriminant function analysis	Discriminant function analysis is a statistical analysis to predict a categorical dependent variable (called a grouping variable) by one or more continuous or binary independent variables (called predictor variables).

Chapter 21. Epilogue: life after discovering statistics

	The original dichotomous discriminant analysis was developed by Sir Ronald Fisher in 1936 It is different from an ANOVA or MANOVA, which is used to predict one (ANOVA) or multiple (MANOVA) continuous dependent variables by one or more independent categorical variables. Discriminant function analysis is useful in determining whether a set of variables is effective in predicting category membership Discriminant analysis is used when groups are known a priori (unlike in cluster analysis).
Dummy variable	In statistics and econometrics, particularly in regression analysis, a dummy variable (also known as an indicator variable) is one that takes the values 0 or 1 to indicate the absence or presence of some categorical effect that may be expected to shift the outcome. For example, in econometric time series analysis, dummy variables may be used to indicate the occurrence of wars, or major strikes. It could thus be thought of as a truth value represented as a numerical value 0 or 1 (as is sometimes done in computer programming).
Ecological validity	Ecological validity is a form of validity in a research study. For a research study to have ecological validity, the methods, materials and setting of the study must approximate the real-world that is being examined. Unlike internal and external validity, ecological validity is not necessary to the overall validity of a study.
Effect size	In statistics, an effect size is a measure of the strength of a phenomenon (for example, the relationship between two variables in a statistical population) or a sample-based estimate of that quantity. An effect size calculated from data is a descriptive statistic that conveys the estimated magnitude of a relationship without making any statement about whether the apparent relationship in the data reflects a true relationship in the population. In that way, effect sizes complement inferential statistics such as p-values.
Error bar	Error bars are a graphical representation of the variability of data and are used on graphs to indicate the error, or uncertainty in a reported measurement. They give a general idea of how accurate a measurement is, or conversely, how far from the reported value the true (error free) value might be. Error bars often represent one standard deviation of uncertainty, one standard error, or a certain confidence interval (e.g., a 95% interval).
Experimentwise error rate	In statistics, during multiple comparisons testing, experimentwise error rate is the probability of at least one false rejection of the null hypothesis over an entire experiment. The α (alpha) that is assigned applies to all of the hypothesis tests as a whole, not individually as in the comparisonwise error rate. In two or higher factorial ANOVAs the experimentwise error rate is higher than the familywise error rate (error within a factor or interaction).
Fisher's exact test	Fisher's exact test is a statistical significance test used in the analysis of contingency tables where sample sizes are small. It is named after its inventor, R. A.

Fisher, and is one of a class of exact tests, so called because the significance of the deviation from a null hypothesis can be calculated exactly, rather than relying on an approximation that becomes exact in the limit as the sample size grows to infinity, as with many statistical tests. Fisher is said to have devised the test following a comment from Muriel Bristol, who claimed to be able to detect whether the tea or the milk was added first to her cup.

| Goodman and Kruskal's lambda | In probability theory and statistics, Goodman & Kruskal's lambda (λ) is a measure of proportional reduction in error in cross tabulation analysis. For any sample with a nominal independent variable and dependent variable (or ones that can be treated nominally), it indicates the extent to which the modal categories and frequencies for each value of the independent variable differ from the overall modal category and frequency, i.e. for all values of the independent variable together. λ can be calculated with the equation $$\lambda = \frac{\varepsilon_1 - \varepsilon_2}{\varepsilon_1}.$$ where ε_1 is the overall non-modal frequency, and ε_2 is the sum of the non-modal frequencies for each value of the independent variable. |

Values for lambda range from zero (no association between independent and dependent variables) to one (perfect association). Weaknesses

Although Goodman and Kruskal's lambda is used to calculate association between variables, it yields a value of 0 (no association) whenever two variables are in accord--that is, when the modal category is the same for all values of the independent variable, even if the modal frequencies or percentages vary.

| Levene's test | In statistics, Levene's test is an inferential statistic used to assess the equality of variances in different samples. Some common statistical procedures assume that variances of the populations from which different samples are drawn are equal. Levene's test assesses this assumption. |

| Familywise error rate | In statistics, familywise error rate is the probability of making one or more false discoveries, or type I errors among all the hypotheses when performing multiple hypotheses tests. FWER definition |

Suppose we have m null hypotheses, denoted by: H_1, H_2, .. H_m. Using a statistical test, each hypothesis is declared significant/non-significant. Summing the test results over H_i will give us the following table and related random variables:• m_0 is the number of true null hypotheses, an unknown parameter• $m - m_0$ is the number of true alternative hypotheses• V is the number of false positives (Type I error)• S is the number of true positives• T is the number of false negatives (Type II error)• U is the number of true negatives• R is the number of rejected null hypotheses• R is an observable random variable, while S, T, U, and

Chapter 21. Epilogue: life after discovering statistics

V are unobservable random variables

The FWER is the probability of making even one type I error In the family,

$$FWER = \Pr(V \geq 1),$$

or equivalently, $FWER = 1 - \Pr(V = 0).$

Thus, by assuring $FWER \leq \alpha,$, the probability of making even one type I error in the family is controlled at level α

A procedure controls the FWER in the weak sense if the FWER control at level α is guaranteed only when all null hypotheses are true (i.e. when $m_0 = m$ so the global null hypothesis is true)

A procedure controls the FWER in the strong sense if the FWER control at level α is guaranteed for any configuration of true and non-true null hypotheses (including the global null hypothesis) The concept of a family

Within the statistical framework, there are several definitions for the term 'family':•First of all, a distinction must be made between exploratory data analysis and confirmatory data analysis: for exploratory analysis - the family constitutes all inferences made and those that potentially could be made, whereas in the case of confirmatory analysis, the family must include only inferences of interest specified prior to the study•Hochberg & Tamhane (1987) define 'family' as 'any collection of inferences for which it is meaningful to take into account some combined measure of error'•According to Cox (1982), a set of inferences should be regarded a family:•To take into account the selection effect due to data dredging•To ensure simultaneous correctness of a set of inferences as to guarantee a correct overall decision

To summarize, a family could best be defined by the potential selective inference that is being faced: A family is the smallest set of items of inference in an analysis, interchangeable about their meaning for the goal of research, from which selection of results for action, presentation or highlighting could be made (Benjamini).

Tukey first coined the term experimentwise error rate and 'per-experiment' error rate for the error rate that the researcher should use as a control level in a multiple hypothesis experiment.

Frequency distribution	In statistics, a frequency distribution is an arrangement of the values that one or more variables take in a sample. Each entry in the table contains the frequency or count of the occurrences of values within a particular group or interval, and in this way, the table summarizes the distribution of values in the sample. Univariate frequency tables

Goodness of fit	The goodness of fit of a statistical model describes how well it fits a set of observations. Measures of goodness of fit typically summarize the discrepancy between observed values and the values expected under the model in question. Such measures can be used in statistical hypothesis testing, e.g. to test for normality of residuals, to test whether two samples are drawn from identical distributions , or whether outcome frequencies follow a specified distribution .
Grand mean	The grand mean is the mean of the means of several subsamples. For example, consider several lots, each containing several items. The items from each lot are sampled for a measure of some variable and the means of the measurements from each lot are computed.
Factorial design	In statistics, a full Factorial design is an experiment whose design consists of two or more factors, each with discrete possible values or 'levels', and whose experimental units take on all possible combinations of these levels across all such factors. A full Factorial design may also be called a fully crossed design. Such an experiment allows studying the effect of each factor on the response variable, as well as the effects of interactions between factors on the response variable.
Growth curve	A growth curve is an empirical model of the evolution of a quantity over time. Growth curves are widely used in biology for quantities such as population size, body height or biomass. Values for the measured property can be plotted on a graph as a function of time.
Harmonic mean	In mathematics, the harmonic mean is one of several kinds of average. Typically, it is appropriate for situations when the average of rates is desired. It is the special case (M^{-1}) of the power mean.
Heteroscedasticity	In statistics, a collection of random variables is heteroscedastic if there are sub-populations that have different variabilities from others. Here 'variability' could be quantified by the variance or any other measure of statistical dispersion. Thus heteroscedasticity is the absence of homoscedasticity.
Histogram	In statistics, a histogram is a graphical representation showing a visual impression of the distribution of data. It is an estimate of the probability distribution of a continuous variable and was first introduced by Karl Pearson. A histogram consists of tabular frequencies, shown as adjacent rectangles, erected over discrete intervals (bins), with an area equal to the frequency of the observations in the interval.
Homogeneity	In statistics, homogeneity and its opposite, heterogeneity, arise in describing the properties of a dataset, or several datasets. They relate to the validity of the often convenient assumption that the statistical properties of any one part of an overall dataset are the same as any other part.

Chapter 21. Epilogue: life after discovering statistics

Homoscedastic	In statistics, a sequence or a vector of random variables is homoscedastic if all random variables in the sequence or vector have the same finite variance. This is also known as homogeneity of variance. The complementary notion is called heteroscedasticity.
Regression	Regression in medicine is a characteristic of diseases to show lighter symptoms without completely disappearing. At a later point, symptoms may return. These symptoms are then called recidive.
Kendall's W	Kendall's W is a non-parametric statistic. It is a normalization of the statistic of the Friedman test, and can be used for assessing agreement among raters. Kendall's W ranges from 0 (no agreement) to 1 (complete agreement).
Kolmogorov-Smirnov test	In statistics, the Kolmogorov-Smirnov test is a nonparametric test for the equality of continuous, one-dimensional probability distributions that can be used to compare a sample with a reference probability distribution (one-sample K-S test), or to compare two samples (two-sample K-S test). The Kolmogorov-Smirnov statistic quantifies a distance between the empirical distribution function of the sample and the cumulative distribution function of the reference distribution, or between the empirical distribution functions of two samples. The null distribution of this statistic is calculated under the null hypothesis that the samples are drawn from the same distribution (in the two-sample case) or that the sample is drawn from the reference distribution (in the one-sample case).
Independent variable	The terms 'dependent variable' and 'Independent variable' are used in similar but subtly different ways in mathematics and statistics as part of the standard terminology in those subjects. They are used to distinguish between two types of quantities being considered, separating them into those available at the start of a process and those being created by it, where the latter (dependent variables) are dependent on the former (Independent variables). The Independent variable is typically the variable being manipulated or changed and the dependent variable is the observed result of the Independent variable being manipulated.
Interaction	In statistics, an interaction may arise when considering the relationship among three or more variables, and describes a situation in which the simultaneous influence of two variables on a third is not additive. Most commonly, interactions are considered in the context of regression analyses. The presence of interactions can have important implications for the interpretation of statistical models.

Interquartile range	In descriptive statistics, the interquartile range also called the midspread or middle fifty, is a measure of statistical dispersion, being equal to the difference between the upper and lower quartiles, $IQR = Q_3 - Q_1$ Use
	Unlike (total) range, the interquartile range has a breakdown point of 25%, and is thus often preferred to the total range.
	The IQR is used to build box plots, simple graphical representations of a probability distribution.
	For a symmetric distribution (where the median equals the midhinge, the average of the first and third quartiles), half the IQR equals the median absolute deviation (MAD).
Intraclass correlation	In statistics, the intraclass correlation is a descriptive statistic that can be used when quantitative measurements are made on units that are organized into groups. It describes how strongly units in the same group resemble each other. While it is viewed as a type of correlation, unlike most other correlation measures it operates on data structured as groups, rather than data structured as paired observations.
Sampling	In statistics and survey methodology, sampling is concerned with the selection of a subset of individuals from within a population to estimate characteristics of the whole population.
	Researchers rarely survey the entire population because the cost of a census is too high. The three main advantages of sampling are that the cost is lower, data collection is faster, and since the data set is smaller it is possible to ensure homogeneity and to improve the accuracy and quality of the data.
M-estimator	In statistics, M-estimators are a broad class of estimators, which are obtained as the minima of sums of functions of the data. Least-squares estimators and many maximum-likelihood estimators are M-estimators. The definition of M-estimators was motivated by robust statistics, which contributed new types of M-estimators.
Mahalanobis distance	In statistics, Mahalanobis distance is a distance measure introduced by P. C. Mahalanobis in 1936. It is based on correlations between variables by which different patterns can be identified and analyzed. It gauges similarity of an unknown sample set to a known one. It differs from Euclidean distance in that it takes into account the correlations of the data set and is scale-invariant.
Kurtosis	In probability theory and statistics, kurtosis is any measure of the 'peakedness' of the probability distribution of a real-valued random variable.

Chapter 21. Epilogue: life after discovering statistics

In a similar way to the concept of skewness, kurtosis is a descriptor of the shape of a probability distribution and, just as for skewness, there are different ways of quantifying it for a theoretical distribution and corresponding ways of estimating it from a sample from a population. There are various interpretations of kurtosis, and of how particular measures should be interpreted; these are primarily peakedness (width of peak), tail weight, and lack of shoulders (distribution primarily peak and tails, not in between).

Levels of measurement	The 'levels of measurement', or scales of measure are expressions that typically refer to the theory of scale types developed by the psychologist Stanley Smith Stevens In that article, Stevens claimed that all measurement in science was conducted using four different types of scales that he called 'nominal', 'ordinal', 'interval' and 'ratio'.
Leverage	In statistics, leverage is a term used in connection with regression analysis and, in particular, in analyses aimed at identifying those observations that are far away from corresponding average predictor values. Leverage points do not necessarily have a large effect on the outcome of fitting regression models. Leverage points are those observations, if any, made at extreme or outlying values of the independent variables such that the lack of neighboring observations means that the fitted regression model will pass close to that particular observation.
Line chart	A line chart is a type of chart which displays information as a series of data points connected by straight line segments. It is a basic type of chart common in many fields. It is an extension of a scatter graph, and is created by connecting a series of points that represent individual measurements with line segments.
Linear model	In statistics, the term linear model is used in different ways according to the context. The most common occurrence is in connection with regression models and the term is often taken as synonymous with linear regression model. However, the term is also used in time series analysis with a different meaning.
Loglinear analysis	Loglinear analysis is a technique used in statistics to examine the relationship between more than two categorical variables. The technique is used for both hypothesis testing and model building. In both these uses, models are tested to find the most parsimonious (i.e., least complex) model that best accounts for the variance in the observed frequencies.
Lower bound	In mathematics, especially in order theory, an upper bound of a subset S of some partially ordered set (P, ≤) is an element of P which is greater than or equal to every element of S. The term lower bound is defined dually as an element of P which is lesser than or equal to every element of S. A set with an upper bound is said to be bounded from above by that bound, a set with a lower bound is said to be bounded from below by that bound.

A subset S of a partially ordered set P may fail to have any bounds or may have many different upper and lower bounds. By transitivity, any element greater than or equal to an upper bound of S is again an upper bound of S, and any element lesser than or equal to any lower bound of S is again a lower bound of S. This leads to the consideration of least upper bounds: (or suprema) and greatest lower bounds (or infima).

Lower quartile	In descriptive statistics, a quartile is any of the three values which divide the sorted data set into four equal parts, so that each part represents one fourth of the sampled population.

In epidemiology, the quartiles are the four ranges defined by the three values discussed here.

· first quartile (designated Q_1) = Lower quartile = cuts off lowest 25% of data = 25th percentile · second quartile (designated Q_2) = median = cuts data set in half = 50th percentile · third quartile (designated Q_3) = upper quartile = cuts off highest 25% of data, or lowest 75% = 75th percentile

The difference between the upper and Lower quartiles(n)left(cfrac{y}{100} ight).' src='../../tx/pod/38e9246c395ff4800c290c59a6fcd09c.png'>

· Case 1: If L is a whole number, then the value will be found halfway between positions L and L+1. · Case 2: If L is a decimal, round up to the nearest whole number. (for example, L = 1.2 becomes 2).

Method 1

· Use the median to divide the ordered data set into two halves.

Main effect	In the design of experiments and analysis of variance, a main effect is the effect of an independent variable on a dependent variable averaging across the levels of any other independent variables. The term is frequently used in the context of factorial designs and regression models to distinguish main effects from interaction effects.

Relative to a a factorial design, under an analysis of variance, a main effect test will test the hypotheses expected such as H0, the null hypothesis.

McNemar's test	In statistics, McNemar's test is a non-parametric method used on nominal data. It is applied to 2 × 2 contingency tables with a dichotomous trait, with matched pairs of subjects, to determine whether the row and column marginal frequencies are equal ('marginal homogeneity'). It is named after Quinn McNemar, who introduced it in 1947. An application of the test in genetics is the transmission disequilibrium test for detecting genetic linkage.

Chapter 21. Epilogue: life after discovering statistics

Monte Carlo method	Monte Carlo methods are a class of computational algorithms that rely on repeated random sampling to compute their results. Monte Carlo methods are often used in computer simulations of physical and mathematical systems. These methods are most suited to calculation by a computer and tend to be used when it is infeasible to compute an exact result with a deterministic algorithm.
Least squares	In mathematics, the idea of least squares can be applied to approximating a given function by a weighted sum of other functions. The best approximation can be defined as that which minimises the difference between the original function and the approximation; for a least-squares approach the quality of the approximation is measured in terms of the squared differences the two. Functional analysis A generalization to approximation of a data set is the approximation of a function by a sum of other functions, usually an orthogonal set: $$f(x) \approx f_n(x) = a_1\phi_1(x) + a_2\phi_2(x) + \cdots + a_n\phi_n(x),$$ with the set of functions { $\phi_j(x)$ } an orthonormal set over the interval of interest, say [a, b].
Maximum likelihood	In statistics, maximum-likelihood estimation (MLE) is a method of estimating the parameters of a statistical model. When applied to a data set and given a statistical model, maximum-likelihood estimation provides estimates for the model's parameters. The method of maximum likelihood corresponds to many well-known estimation methods in statistics.
Maximum likelihood estimation	Maximum likelihood estimation is a popular statistical method used for fitting a statistical model to data, and providing estimates for the model's parameters. The method of maximum likelihood corresponds to many well-known estimation methods in statistics. For example, suppose you are interested in the heights of Americans.
Median	In probability theory and statistics, a median is described as the numerical value separating the higher half of a sample, a population, or a probability distribution, from the lower half. The median of a finite list of numbers can be found by arranging all the observations from lowest value to highest value and picking the middle one. If there is an even number of observations, then there is no single middle value; the median is then usually defined to be the mean of the two middle values.
Median test	In statistics, Mood's median test is a special case of Pearson's chi-squared test. It is a nonparametric test that tests the null hypothesis that the medians of the populations from which two samples are drawn are identical.

Meta-analysis	In statistics, a meta-analysis refers to methods focused on contrasting and combining results from different studies, in the hope of identifying patterns among study results, sources of disagreement among those results, or other interesting relationships that may come to light in the context of multiple studies. In its simplest form, this is normally by identification of a common measure of effect size, of which a weighted average might be the output of a meta-analysis. The weighting might be related to sample sizes within the individual studies.
Hypothetico-deductive model	The hypothetico-deductive model, first so-named by William Whewell, is a proposed description of scientific method. According to it, scientific inquiry proceeds by formulating a hypothesis in a form that could conceivably be falsified by a test on observable data. A test that could and does run contrary to predictions of the hypothesis is taken as a falsification of the hypothesis.
Mode	The mode is the number that appears most often in a set of numbers. Like the statistical mean and median, the mode is a way of capturing important information about a random variable or a population in a single quantity. The mode is in general different from the mean and median, and may be very different for strongly skewed distributions.
Moderation	Moderation in Regression Analysis In statistics, moderation occurs when the relationship between two variables depends on a third variable. The third variable is referred to as the moderator variable or simply the moderator . The effect of a moderating variable is characterized statistically as an interaction; that is, a qualitative (e.g., sex, race, class) or quantitative (e.g., level of reward) variable that affects the direction and/or strength of the relation between dependent and independent variables.
Moderator variable	In statistics, moderation occurs when the relationship between two variables depends on a third variable. The third variable is referred to as the Moderator variable or simply the moderator. The effect of a moderating variable is characterized statistically as an interaction; that is, a qualitative (e.g., sex, race, class) or quantitative (e.g., level of reward) variable that affects the direction and/or strength of the relation between dependent and independent variables.
Multicollinearity	Multicollinearity is a statistical phenomenon in which two or more predictor variables in a multiple regression model are highly correlated. In this situation the coefficient estimates may change erratically in response to small changes in the model or the data. Multicollinearity does not reduce the predictive power or reliability of the model as a whole, at least within the sample data themselves; it only affects calculations regarding individual predictors.
Normal distribution	In probability theory, the normal distribution is a continuous probability distribution that has a bell-shaped probability density function, known as the Gaussian function or informally the bell curve:

Chapter 21. Epilogue: life after discovering statistics

$$f(x; \mu, \sigma^2) = \frac{1}{\sigma\sqrt{2\pi}} e^{-\frac{1}{2}\left(\frac{x-\mu}{\sigma}\right)^2}$$

The parameter μ is the mean or expectation (location of the peak) and $\sigma^{?2}$ is the variance. σ is known as the standard deviation. The distribution with μ = 0 and $\sigma^{?2}$ = 1 is called the standard normal distribution or the unit normal distribution.

Sphericity	Sphericity is a measure of how spherical (round) an object is. As such, it is a specific example of a compactness measure of a shape. Defined by Wadell in 1935, the sphericity, Ψ, of a particle is: the ratio of the surface area of a sphere (with the same volume as the given particle) to the surface area of the particle: $$\Psi = \frac{\pi^{\frac{1}{3}}(6V_p)^{\frac{2}{3}}}{A_p}$$ where V_p is volume of the particle and A_p is the surface area of the particle.
Factorial ANOVA	Factorial ANOVA is used when the experimenter wants to study the effects of two or more treatment variables. The most commonly used type of Factorial ANOVA is the 2^2 (read 'two by two') design, where there are two independent variables and each variable has two levels or distinct values. However, such use of ANOVA for analysis of 2^k factorial designs and fractional factorial designs is 'confusing and makes little sense'; instead it is suggested to refer the value of the effect divided by its standard error to a t-table. Factorial ANOVA can also be multi-level such as 3^3, etc. or higher order such as 2×2×2, etc.. Since the introduction of data analytic software, the utilization of higher order designs and analyses has become quite common.
Multimodal distribution	In statistics, a bimodal distribution is a continuous probability distribution with two different modes. These appear as distinct peaks (local maxima) in the probability density function.
	More generally, a multimodal distribution is a continuous probability distribution with two or more modes.
Multinomial logistic regression	In statistics, a multinomial logistic regression model, also known as softmax regression or multinomial logit, is a regression model which generalizes logistic regression by allowing more than two discrete outcomes. That is, it is a model that is used to predict the probabilities of the different possible outcomes of a categorically distributed dependent variable, given a set of independent variables (which may be real-valued, binary-valued, categorical-valued, etc).. The use of the term 'multinomial' in the name arises from the common conflation between the categorical and multinomial distributions, as explained in the relevant articles.

Multiple regression	In statistics, linear regression is an approach to modeling the relationship between a scalar dependent variable y and one or more explanatory variables denoted X. The case of one explanatory variable is called simple regression. More than one explanatory variable is multiple regression. (This in turn should be distinguished from multivariate linear regression, where multiple correlated dependent variables are predicted, rather than a single scalar variable).
Multivariate analysis	Multivariate analysis is based on the statistical principle of multivariate statistics, which involves observation and analysis of more than one statistical outcome variable at a time. In design and analysis, the technique is used to perform trade studies across multiple dimensions while taking into account the effects of all variables on the responses of interest.
	Uses for multivariate analysis include:•Design for capability (also known as capability-based design)•Inverse design, where any variable can be treated as an independent variable•Analysis of Alternatives (AoA), the selection of concepts to fulfill a customer need•Analysis of concepts with respect to changing scenarios•Identification of critical design drivers and correlations across hierarchical levels
	Multivariate analysis can be complicated by the desire to include physics-based analysis to calculate the effects of variables for a hierarchical 'system-of-systems.' Often, studies that wish to use multivariate analysis are stalled by the dimensionality of the problem.
Multivariate analysis of variance	Multivariate analysis of variance is a statistical test procedure for comparing multivariate (population) means of several groups. Unlike ANOVA, it uses the variance-covariance between variables in testing the statistical significance of the mean differences.
	It is a generalized form of univariate analysis of variance (ANOVA).
Ordinary least squares	In statistics, ordinary least squares or linear least squares is a method for estimating the unknown parameters in a linear regression model. This method minimizes the sum of squared vertical distances between the observed responses in the dataset and the responses predicted by the linear approximation. The resulting estimator can be expressed by a simple formula, especially in the case of a single regressor on the right-hand side.
Outlier	In statistics, an outlier is an observation that is numerically distant from the rest of the data. Grubbs defined an outlier as:'
	An outlying observation, or outlier, is one that appears to deviate markedly from other members of the sample in which it occurs. '

Chapter 21. Epilogue: life after discovering statistics

Overdispersion	In statistics, overdispersion is the presence of greater variability (statistical dispersion) in a data set than would be expected based on a given simple statistical model. A common task in applied statistics is choosing a parametric model to fit a given set of empirical observations. This necessitates an assessment of the fit of the chosen model.
Parameter	Parameter can be interpreted in mathematics, logic, linguistics, environmental science and other disciplines. In its common meaning, the term is used to identify a characteristic, a feature, a measurable factor that can help in defining a particular system. It is an important element to take into consideration for the evaluation or for the comprehension of an event, a project or any situation.
P-P plot	In statistics, a P-P plot is a probability plot for assessing how closely two data sets agree, which plots the two cumulative distribution functions against each other. The Q-Q plot is more widely used, but they are both referred to as 'the' probability plot, and are potentially confused. A P-P plot plots two cumulative distribution functions (cdfs) against each other: given two probability distributions, with cdfs 'F' and 'G', it plots $(F(z), G(z))$ as z ranges from $-\infty$ to ∞. As a cdf has range [0,1], the domain of this parametric graph is $(-\infty, \infty)$ and the range is the unit square $[0, 1] \times [0, 1]$. Thus for input z the output is the pair of numbers giving what percentage of f and what percentage of g fall at or below z.
Precision	In statistics, the term precision can mean a quantity defined in a specific way. This is in addition to its more general meaning in the contexts of accuracy and precision and of precision and recall. There can be differences in usage of the term for particular statistical models but, in general statistical usage, the precision is defined to be the reciprocal of the variance, while the precision matrix is the matrix inverse of the covariance matrix.
Semipartial correlation	Semipartial correlation is the correlation the independent with the dependent, controlling only the independent variable for control variables.

Percentile	In statistics and the social sciences, a percentile is the value of a variable below which a certain percent of observations fall. For example, the 20th percentile is the value (or score) below which 20 percent of the observations may be found. The term percentile and the related term percentile rank are often used in the reporting of scores from norm-referenced tests.
Polynomial	In mathematics, a polynomial is an expression of finite length constructed from variables (also known as indeterminates) and constants, using only the operations of addition, subtraction, multiplication, and non-negative integer exponents. For example, $x^2 - 4x + 7$ is a polynomial, but $x^2 - 4/x + 7x^{3/2}$ is not, because its second term involves division by the variable x (4/x) and because its third term contains an exponent that is not a whole number (3/2). The term 'polynomial' indicates a simplified algebraic form such that all polynomials are similarly simple in complexity (cf.
Post hoc	Post hoc ergo propter hoc, Latin for 'after this, therefore because of this', is a logical fallacy (of the questionable cause variety) that states 'Since that event followed this one, that event must have been caused by this one.' It is often shortened to simply post hoc. It is subtly different from the fallacy cum hoc ergo propter hoc, in which two things or events occur simultaneously or the chronological ordering is insignificant or unknown, also referred to as false cause, coincidental correlation, or correlation not causation. Post hoc is a particularly tempting error because temporal sequence appears to be integral to causality.
Practice effect	Practice effect is a systematic change (increase or decrease) in performance over a series of treatment conditions in a repeated measures (within-subjects) designt. A potential source of error usually neutralized by using a counterbalancing design.
Q-Q plot	In statistics, a Q-Q plot is a probability plot, which is a graphical method for comparing two probability distributions by plotting their quantiles against each other. First, the set of intervals for the quantiles are chosen. A point (x,y) on the plot corresponds to one of the quantiles of the second distribution (y-coordinate) plotted against the same quantile of the first distribution (x-coordinate).
Density function	In probability theory, a probability density function or density of a continuous random variable, is a function that describes the relative likelihood for this random variable to take on a given value. The probability for the random variable to fall within a particular region is given by the integral of this variable's density over the region. The probability density function is nonnegative everywhere, and its integral over the entire space is equal to one.
Linear regression	In statistics, linear regression is an approach to modeling the relationship between a scalar dependent variable y and one or more explanatory variables denoted X.

Chapter 21. Epilogue: life after discovering statistics

	The case of one explanatory variable is called simple regression. More than one explanatory variable is multiple regression. (This in turn should be distinguished from multivariate linear regression, where multiple correlated dependent variables are predicted, rather than a single scalar variable).
Outcome	In game theory, an outcome is a set of moves or strategies taken by the players, or it is their payoffs resulting from the actions or strategies taken by all players. The two are complementary in that, given knowledge of the set of strategies of all players, the final state of the game is known, as are any relevant payoffs. In a game where chance or a random event is involved, the outcome is not known from only the set of strategies, but is only realized when the random event(s) are realized.
Predictive validity	In psychometrics, predictive validity is the extent to which a score on a scale or test predicts scores on some criterion measure.
	For example, the validity of a cognitive test for job performance is the correlation between test scores and, for example, supervisor performance ratings. Such a cognitive test would have predictive validity if the observed correlation were statistically significant.
Predictor variable	The predictor variable is manipulated by the experimenter. By attempting to isolate all other factors, one can determine the influence of the independent variable on the dependent variable.
Principal	In commercial law, a principal is a person, legal or natural, who authorizes an agent to act to create one or more legal relationships with a third party. This branch of law is called agency and relies on the common law proposition qui facit per alium, facit per se .
	It is a parallel concept to vicarious liability and strict liability (in which one person is held liable for the acts or omissions of another) in criminal law or torts.
Principal component	Principal component analysis (PCA) involves a mathematical procedure that transforms a number of possibly correlated variables into a smaller number of uncorrelated variables called principal components. The first principal component accounts for as much of the variability in the data as possible, and each succeeding component accounts for as much of the remaining variability as possible. Depending on the field of application, it is also named the discrete Karhunen-Loève transform (KLT), the Hotelling transform or proper orthogonal decomposition (POD).
Principal components analysis	Principal components analysis is a technique for simplifying a dataset.

Probability density function	In probability theory, a probability density function or density of a continuous random variable, is a function that describes the relative likelihood for this random variable to take on a given value. The probability for the random variable to fall within a particular region is given by the integral of this variable's density over the region. The probability density function is nonnegative everywhere, and its integral over the entire space is equal to one.
Probability distribution	In probability and statistics, a probability distribution assigns a probability to each of the possible outcomes of a random experiment. Examples are found in experiments whose sample space is non-numerical, where the distribution would be a categorical distribution; experiments whose sample space is encoded by discrete random variables, where the distribution is a probability mass function; and experiments with sample spaces encoded by continuous random variables, where the distribution is a probability density function. More complex experiments, such as those involving stochastic processes defined in continuous-time, may demand the use of more general probability measures.
Quantile	Quantiles are points taken at regular intervals from the cumulative distribution function (CDF) of a random variable. Dividing ordered data into q essentially equal-sized data subsets is the motivation for q-quantiles; the quantiles are the data values marking the boundaries between consecutive subsets. Put another way, the kth q-quantile for a random variable is the value x such that the probability that the random variable will be less than x is at most k/q and the probability that the random variable will be more than x is at most $$(q-k)/q = 1 - (k/q).$$
Random effects	In statistics, a random effect(s) model, also called a variance components model, is a kind of hierarchical linear model. It assumes that the dataset being analysed consists of a hierarchy of different populations whose differences relate to that hierarchy. In econometrics, random effects models are used in the analysis of hierarchical or panel data when one assumes no fixed effects (i.e. no individual effects).
Random variable	In probability and statistics, a random variable is subject to variations due to chance (i.e. randomness, in a mathematical sense). As opposed to other mathematical variables, a random variable conceptually does not have a single, fixed value (even if unknown); rather, it can take on a set of possible different values, each with an associated probability. A random variable's possible values might represent the possible outcomes of a yet-to-be-performed experiment or an event that has not happened yet, or the potential values of a past experiment or event whose already-existing value is uncertain (e.g. as a result of incomplete information or imprecise measurements).

Chapter 21. Epilogue: life after discovering statistics

Reliability	In statistics, reliability refers to the consistency of a measure. A measure is said to have a high reliability if it produces consistent results under consistent conditions. For example, measurements of people's height and weight are often extremely reliable.
Shapiro-Wilk test	In statistics, the Shapiro-Wilk test tests the null hypothesis that a sample $x_1, .. \, x_n$ came from a normally distributed population. It was published in 1965 by Samuel Shapiro and Martin Wilk.

The test statistic is:
$$W = \frac{\left(\sum_{i=1}^{n} a_i x_{(i)} \right)^2}{\sum_{i=1}^{n} (x_i - \overline{x})^2}$$

where• $x_{(i)}$ (with parentheses enclosing the subscript index i) is the ith order statistic, i.e., the ith-smallest number in the sample;• $\overline{x} = (x_1 + \ldots + x_n)/n$ is the sample mean;•the constants a_i are given by
$$(a_1, \ldots, a_n) = \frac{m^\top V^{-1}}{(m^\top V^{-1} V^{-1} m)^{1/2}}$$

$m = (m_1, \ldots, m_n)^\top$ and $m_1, .. \, m_n$ are the expected values of the order statistics of independent and identically distributed random variables sampled from the standard normal distribution, and V is the covariance matrix of those order statistics.

The user may reject the null hypothesis if W is too small.

Residual sum of squares	In statistics, the residual sum of squares is the sum of squares of residuals. It is also known as the sum of squared residuals (SSR) or the sum of squared errors of prediction (SSE). It is a measure of the discrepancy between the data and an estimation model.
Residual	Loosely speaking, a residual is the error in a result. To be precise, suppose we want to find x such that $f(x) = b.$

Given an approximation x_0 of x, the residual is $b - f(x_0)$

whereas the error is $x_0 - x.$

If we do not know x, we cannot compute the error but we can compute the residual. Residual of the approximation of a function

Similar terminology is used dealing with differential, integral and functional equations.

Rotation	In geometry and linear algebra, a rotation is a transformation in a plane or in space that describes the motion of a rigid body around a fixed point.

A rotation is different from a translation, which has no fixed points, and from a reflection, which 'flips' the bodies it is transforming. A rotation and the above-mentioned transformations are isometries; they leave the distance between any two points unchanged after the transformation.

Sampling distribution
In statistics, a sampling distribution is the probability distribution of a given statistic based on a random sample. Sampling distributions are important in statistics because they provide a major simplification on the route to statistical inference. More specifically, they allow analytical considerations to be based on the sampling distribution of a statistic, rather than on the joint probability distribution of all the individual sample values.

Shrinkage
In statistics, shrinkage has two meanings:•In relation to the general observation that, in regression analysis, a fitted relationship appears to perform less well on a new data set than on the data set used for fitting. In particular the value of the coefficient of determination 'shrinks'. This idea is complementary to overfitting and, separately, to the standard adjustment made in the coefficient of determination to compensate for the subjunctive effects of further sampling, like controlling for the potential of new explanatory terms improving the model by chance: that is, the adjustment formula itself provides 'shrinkage.' But the adjustment formula yields an artificial shrinkage, in contrast to the first definition.•To describe general types of estimators, or the effects of some types of estimation, whereby a naive or raw estimate is improved by combining it with other information..

Sign test
In statistics, the sign test can be used to test the hypothesis that there is 'no difference in medians' between the continuous distributions of two random variables X and Y, in the situation when we can draw paired samples from X and Y. It is a non-parametric test which makes very few assumptions about the nature of the distributions under test - this means that it has very general applicability but may lack the statistical power of other tests such as the paired-samples t-test or the Wilcoxon signed-rank test. Method

Let $p = \Pr(X > Y)$, and then test the null hypothesis H_0: $p = 0.50$. In other words, the null hypothesis states that given a random pair of measurements (x_i, y_i), then x_i and y_i are equally likely to be larger than the other.

To test the null hypothesis, independent pairs of sample data are collected from the populations $\{(x_1, y_1), (x_2, y_2), .$

Simple effect
A simple effect of an independent variable is the effect at a single level of another variable. Often they are computed following a significant interaction.

Sobel test
In statistics, the Sobel test is a method of testing the significance of a mediation effect. The test is based on the work of Michael E. Sobel, a sociology professor at Columbia University in New York, NY.

Chapter 21. Epilogue: life after discovering statistics

	In mediation, the relationship between the independent variable and the dependent variable is hypothesized to be an indirect effect that exists due to the influence of a third variable (the mediator). As a result when the mediator is included in a regression analysis model with the independent variable, the effect of the independent variable is reduced and the effect of the mediator remains significant.
Spearman's rank correlation coefficient	In statistics, Spearman's rank correlation coefficient is a non-parametric measure of statistical dependence between two variables. It assesses how well the relationship between two variables can be described using a monotonic function. If there are no repeated data values, a perfect Spearman correlation of +1 or −1 occurs when each of the variables is a perfect monotone function of the other.
Singularity	In mathematics, a singularity is in general a point at which a given mathematical object is not defined, such as differentiability.
Split-half reliability	As the name suggests, split-half reliability is a coefficient obtained by dividing a test into halves, correlating the scores on each half, and then correcting for length (longer tests tend to be more reliable).
Standard deviation	In statistics and probability theory, standard deviation shows how much variation or 'dispersion' exists from the average (mean, or expected value). A low standard deviation indicates that the data points tend to be very close to the mean; high standard deviation indicates that the data points are spread out over a large range of values.
	The standard deviation of a random variable, statistical population, data set, or probability distribution is the square root of its variance.
Standard error	The standard error is the standard deviation of the sampling distribution of a statistic. The term may also be used to refer to an estimate of that standard deviation, derived from a particular sample used to compute the estimate.
	For example, the sample mean is the usual estimator of a population mean.
Stepwise regression	In statistics, stepwise regression includes regression models in which the choice of predictive variables is carried out by an automatic procedure. Usually, this takes the form of a sequence of F-tests, but other techniques are possible, such as t-tests, adjusted R-square, Akaike information criterion, Bayesian information criterion, Mallows' Cp, or false discovery rate.

The main approaches are:•Forward selection, which involves starting with no variables in the model, trying out the variables one by one and including them if they are 'statistically significant'.•Backward elimination, which involves starting with all candidate variables and testing them one by one for statistical significance, deleting any that are not significant.•Methods that are a combination of the above, testing at each stage for variables to be included or excluded.

A widely used algorithm was first proposed by Efroymson (1960).

T-statistic	In statistics, the t-statistic is a ratio of the departure of an estimated parameter from its notional value and its standard error. It is used in hypothesis testing, for example in the Student's t-test, in the augmented Dickey-Fuller test, and in bootstrapping. Let $\hat{\beta}$ be an estimator of parameter β in some statistical model.
Test statistic	In statistical hypothesis testing, a hypothesis test is typically specified in terms of a test statistic, which is a function of the sample; it is considered as a numerical summary of a set of data that reduces the data to one or a small number of values that can be used to perform a hypothesis test. Given a null hypothesis and a test statistic T, we can specify a 'null value' T_0 such that values of T close to T_0 present the strongest evidence in favor of the null hypothesis, whereas values of T far from T_0 present the strongest evidence against the null hypothesis. An important property of a test statistic is that we must be able to determine its sampling distribution under the null hypothesis, which allows us to calculate p-values.
Repeatability	Repeatability is the variation in measurements taken by a single person or instrument on the same item and under the same conditions. A less-than-perfect test-retest reliability causes test-retest variability. Such variability can be caused by, for example, intra-individual variability and intra-observer variability.
Total sum of squares	In statistical data analysis the total sum of squares is a quantity that appears as part of a standard way of presenting results of such analyses. It is defined as being the sum, over all observations, of the squared differences of each observation from the overall mean. In statistical linear models, (particularly in standard regression models), the TSS is the sum of the squares of the difference of the dependent variable and its grand mean: $\sum_{i=1}^{n} (y_i - \bar{y})^2$. Where: $\bar{y}$ is the mean.

Chapter 21. Epilogue: life after discovering statistics

Truncated mean	A truncated mean is a statistical measure of central tendency, much like the mean and median. It involves the calculation of the mean after discarding given parts of a probability distribution or sample at the high and low end, and typically discarding an equal amount of both.
	For most statistical applications, 5 to 25 percent of the ends are discarded.
Two-tailed test	The two-tailed test is a statistical test used in inference, in which a given statistical hypothesis, H_0 (the null hypothesis), will be rejected when the value of the test statistic is either sufficiently small or sufficiently large. This contrasts with a one-tailed test, in which only one of the rejection regions 'sufficiently small' or 'sufficiently large' is preselected according to the alternative hypothesis being selected, and the hypothesis is rejected only if the test statistic satisfies that criterion. Alternative names are one-sided and two-sided tests.
	However, the terminology is extended to tests relating to distributions other than normal. In general a test is called two-tailed if the null hypothesis is rejected for values of the test statistic falling into either tail of its sampling distribution, and it is called one-sided or one-tailed if the null hypothesis is rejected only for values of the test statistic falling into one specified tail of its sampling distribution. For example, if the alternative hypothesis is $\mu \neq 42.5$, rejecting the null hypothesis of $\mu = 42.5$ for small or for large values of the sample mean, the test is called 'two-tailed' or 'two-sided'. If the alternative hypothesis is $\mu > 1.4$, rejecting the null hypothesis of $\mu \leq 1.4$ only for large values of the sample mean, it is then called 'one-tailed' or 'one-sided'.
	If the distribution from which the samples are derived is considered to be normal, Gaussian, or bell-shaped, then the test is referred to as a one- or two-tailed T test. If the test is performed using the actual population mean and variance, rather than an estimate from a sample, it would be called a one- or two-tailed Z test.
Unique variance	Unique variance is the variance of a variable which is not explained by common factors. It is composed of specific and error variance.
Third quartile	The third quartile is designated as Q_3. The upper quartile cuts off highest 25% of data or lowest 75%.
Mann-Whitney U	In statistics, the Mann-Whitney U test is a non-parametric statistical hypothesis test for assessing whether one of two samples of independent observations tends to have larger values than the other. It is one of the most well-known non-parametric significance tests.

CHAPTER HIGHLIGHTS & NOTES: KEY TERMS, PEOPLE, PLACES, CONCEPTS

Wilcoxon signed-rank test	The Wilcoxon signed-rank test is a non-parametric statistical hypothesis test used when comparing two related samples, matched samples, or repeated measurements on a single sample to assess whether their population mean ranks differ (i.e. it is a paired difference test). It can be used as an alternative to the paired Student's t-test, t-test for matched pairs, or the t-test for dependent samples when the population cannot be assumed to be normally distributed.
	The test is named for Frank Wilcoxon (1892-1965) who, in a single paper, proposed both it and the rank-sum test for two independent samples (Wilcoxon, 1945).
Continuity correction	In probability theory, if a random variable X has a binomial distribution with parameters n and p, i.e., X is distributed as the number of 'successes' in n independent Bernoulli trials with probability p of success on each trial, then $P(X \leq x) = P(X < x+1)$
	for any x ∈ {0, 1, 2, ... n}. If np and n(1 − p) are large (sometimes taken to mean ≥ 5), then the probability above is fairly well approximated by $P(Y \leq x + 1/2)$
	where Y is a normally distributed random variable with the same expected value and the same variance as X, i.e., E(Y) = np and var(Y) = np(1 − p). This addition of 1/2 to x is a continuity correction.
Variance inflation factor	In statistics, the variance inflation factor quantifies the severity of multicollinearity in an ordinary least squares regression analysis. It provides an index that measures how much the variance (the square of the estimate's standard deviation) of an estimated regression coefficient is increased because of collinearity.
	Consider the following linear model with k independent variables: $Y = \beta_0 + \beta_1 X_1 + \beta_2 X_2 + ... + \beta_k X_k + \varepsilon$.
	The standard error of the estimate of β_j is the square root of the j+1, j+1 element of $s^2(X'X)^{-1}$, where s is the root mean squared error (RMSE) (note that $RMSE^2$ is an unbiased estimator of the true variance of the error term, σ^2); X is the regression design matrix - a matrix such that $X_{i,\,j+1}$ is the value of the jth independent variable for the ith case or observation, and such that $X_{i,\,1}$ equals 1 for all i.
Critical value	Critical value may refer to: Differential topology
	In differential topology, a critical value of a differentiable function $f : M \rightarrow N$ between differentiable manifolds is the image (value) $f(x)$ in N of a critical point x in M.
	The basic result on critical values is Sard's lemma.

Chapter 21. Epilogue: life after discovering statistics

The set of critical values can be quite irregular; but in Morse theory it becomes important to consider real-valued functions on a manifold M, such that the set of critical values is in fact finite. The theory of Morse functions shows that there are many such functions; and that they are even typical, or generic in the sense of Baire category.

Student t distribution

The Student t distribution is a probability distribution that arises in the problem of estimating the mean of a normally distributed population when the sample size is small. It is the basis of the popular Student's t-tests for the statistical significance of the difference between two sample means, and for confidence intervals for the difference between two population means.

F-distribution

In probability theory and statistics, the F-distribution is a continuous probability distribution. It is also known as Snedecor's F-distribution or the Fisher-Snedecor distribution (after R.A. Fisher and George W. Snedecor). The F-distribution arises frequently as the null distribution of a test statistic, most notably in the analysis of variance.

If a random variable X has an F-distribution with parameters d_1 and d_2, we write $X \sim F(d_1, d_2)$. Then the probability density function for X is given by

$$f(x; d_1, d_2) = \frac{\sqrt{\frac{(d_1\,x)^{d_1}\,d_2^{d_2}}{(d_1\,x + d_2)^{d_1 + d_2}}}}{x\,\mathrm{B}\left(\frac{d_1}{2}, \frac{d_2}{2}\right)}$$

$$= \frac{1}{\mathrm{B}\left(\frac{d_1}{2}, \frac{d_2}{2}\right)} \left(\frac{d_1}{d_2}\right)^{\frac{d_1}{2}} x^{\frac{d_1}{2}-1} \left(1 + \frac{d_1}{d_2} x\right)^{-\frac{d_1 + d_2}{2}}$$

for real x ≥ 0. Here B is the beta function. In many applications, the parameters d_1 and d_2 are positive integers, but the distribution is well-defined for positive real values of these parameters.

1. In statistics, _____ is used to test if k samples are from populations with equal variances. Equal variances across samples is called homoscedasticity or homogeneity of variances. Some statistical tests, for example the analysis of variance, assume that variances are equal across groups or samples.

   a. Bartlett's test
   b. 1-factor
   c. 4-dimensional Euclidean space
   d. Bacterial growth

2. In probability theory and statistics, _____ is any measure of the 'peakedness' of the probability distribution of a real-valued random variable. In a similar way to the concept of skewness, _____ is a descriptor of the shape of a probability distribution and, just as for skewness, there are different ways of quantifying it for a theoretical distribution and corresponding ways of estimating it from a sample from a population. There are various interpretations of _____, and of how particular measures should be interpreted; these are primarily peakedness (width of peak), tail weight, and lack of shoulders (distribution primarily peak and tails, not in between).

   a. Skewness
   b. Airfoil
   c. Algebraic element
   d. Kurtosis

3. In statistics, the number of _____ is the number of values in the final calculation of a statistic that are free to vary.

   Estimates of statistical parameters can be based upon different amounts of information or data. The number of independent pieces of information that go into the estimate of a parameter is called the _____ (df).

   a. Deviation
   b. Degrees of freedom
   c. Floor effect
   d. Grand mean

4. . _____ is a statistical analysis to predict a categorical dependent variable (called a grouping variable) by one or more continuous or binary independent variables (called predictor variables). The original dichotomous discriminant analysis was developed by Sir Ronald Fisher in 1936 It is different from an ANOVA or MANOVA, which is used to predict one (ANOVA) or multiple (MANOVA) continuous dependent variables by one or more independent categorical variables. _____ is useful in determining whether a set of variables is effective in predicting category membership

   Discriminant analysis is used when groups are known a priori (unlike in cluster analysis).

   a. 1-factor
   b. clothoids
   c. Discriminant function analysis

Chapter 21. Epilogue: life after discovering statistics

5. In statistics, a _____ model, also known as softmax regression or multinomial logit, is a regression model which generalizes logistic regression by allowing more than two discrete outcomes. That is, it is a model that is used to predict the probabilities of the different possible outcomes of a categorically distributed dependent variable, given a set of independent variables (which may be real-valued, binary-valued, categorical-valued, etc).. The use of the term 'multinomial' in the name arises from the common conflation between the categorical and multinomial distributions, as explained in the relevant articles.

  a. Neural network
  b. Multinomial logistic regression
  c. Parameter identification problem
  d. Poisson regression

1. a
2. d
3. b
4. c
5. b

You can take the complete Chapter Practice Test

for Chapter 21. Epilogue: life after discovering statistics
on all key terms, persons, places, and concepts.

Online 99 Cents

http://www.epub27.31.21776.21.cram101.com/

Use www.Cram101.com for all your study needs

including Cram101's online interactive problem solving labs in

chemistry, statistics, mathematics, and more.

Other Cram101 e-Books and Tests

Want More?
Cram101.com...

Cram101.com provides the outlines and highlights of your
textbooks, just like this e-StudyGuide, but also gives you the
PRACTICE TESTS, and other exclusive study tools for all of your
textbooks.

Learn More. *Just click*
http://www.cram101.com/

Lightning Source UK Ltd.
Milton Keynes UK
UKOW012136060513

210241UK00003B/37/P